31143011561975
616.8522 Cooper, H
Cooper, Hattie C..
Thriving with social
anxiety : daily
strategies for overcoming
anxiety, building self

D0197119

Main

Thriving with Social Anxiety

DISCARDED
Richmond Public Library

Copyright © 2014 by Althea Press, Berkeley, California.

No part of this publication may be reproduced, stored in a retrieval system, or transmitted in any form or by any means, electronic, mechanical, photocopying, recording, scanning, or otherwise, except as permitted under Sections 107 or 108 of the 1976 US Copyright Act, without the prior written permission of the Publisher. Requests to the Publisher for permission should be addressed to the Permissions Department, Althea Press, 918 Parker St, Suite A-12, Berkeley, CA 94710.

Limit of Liability/Disclaimer of Warranty: The Publisher and the author make no representations or warranties with respect to the accuracy or completeness of the contents of this work and specifically disclaim all warranties, including without limitation warranties of fitness for a particular purpose. No warranty may be created or extended by sales or promotional materials. The advice and strategies contained herein may not be suitable for every situation. This work is sold with the understanding that the Publisher is not engaged in rendering medical, legal, or other professional advice or services. If professional assistance is required, the services of a competent professional person should be sought. Neither the Publisher nor the author shall be liable for damages arising herefrom. The fact that an individual, organization, or website is referred to in this work as a citation and/or potential source of further information does not mean that the author or the Publisher endorses the information the individual, organization, or website may provide or recommendations they/it may make. Further, readers should be aware that websites listed in this work may have changed or disappeared between when this work was written and when it is read.

For general information on our other products and services or to obtain technical support, please contact our Customer Care Department within the United States at (866) 744-2665, or outside the United States at (510) 253-0500.

Althea Press publishes its books in a variety of electronic and print formats. Some content that appears in print may not be available in electronic books, and vice versa.

TRADEMARKS: Althea Press and the Althea Press logo are trademarks or registered trademarks of Callisto Media, Inc., and/or its affiliates, in the United States and other countries, and may not be used without written permission. All other trademarks are the property of their respective owners. Althea Press is not associated with any product or vendor mentioned in this book.

ISBN: Print 978-1-62315-623-7 | eBook 978-1-62315-624-4

DAILY
STRATEGIES
FOR

overcoming
anxiety

building
self-
confidence

Thriving
with
Social
Anxiety

HATTIE C. COOPER

with a foreword by Kyle MacDonald

ALTHEA
PRESS

QUICK START GUIDE

Need a quick overview
of social anxiety?
Start with part I

Interested in Cognitive
Behavioral Therapy (CBT)?
Turn to chapter 4

Curious about mindfulness?
Chapter 5 has answers

Ready to try exposure therapy?
Flip to chapter 6 for
safe approaches

Interested in meditation?
Find guidance in chapter 7

Seeking to build confidence
and assertiveness?
Read through chapter 9

Prefer a natural path?
Chapter 11 includes
recipes and remedies

Contents

Foreword

In 15 years of clinical practice, I have found that my clients who struggle with social anxiety are without question some of the most pleasant people I've ever met . . . they just don't know it.

People who feel anxious and shy in social situations are often more intelligent, more empathic, and more sensitive to other people's emotional states. And, although in many ways these traits cause the problems associated with social anxiety, they also make those who display them really good company. Intelligence, empathy, and sensitivity are desirable traits in any friend or partner. In fact, a major reason I designed an entire treatment system to help people overcome their social anxiety is because I truly enjoy helping people realize that they can be great partners, great friends, and great company.

Social anxiety grows from experiences of feeling or being told that you are weird, out of place, strange, or wrong. Anxiety can develop as a result of trauma or bullying, or through a lack of sensitive, attuned parenting. And when someone with an emotionally sensitive temperament—or someone who has an innate tendency to avoid situations that provoke anxiety and strong emotions—goes through these experiences, they may become afraid to face similar situations. This fear is fueled by the assumption that other people cause harm, and it grows into anxiety when a person's feelings about themselves become dependent on their interactions with others.

In simple terms, all successful treatments for social anxiety involve helping people see reality more clearly and allowing them to distinguish the distortions of inaccurate beliefs and intense feelings. Techniques such as mindfulness, cognitive behavioral therapy (CBT), and introspective psychodynamic psychotherapy all help by clarifying the truth behind someone's anxiety and developing an awareness of how to counteract its effects.

So what is that truth? Often, it's that you're a much better, more appealing person than you can comprehend and that other people are largely just as conflicted as you, but may be a little better at hiding it. Feelings aren't harmful; they provide necessary information about the world around us. If other people intentionally put you down and try to provoke strong emotions in you, it's often because those other people are insecure and tend toward bullying behavior to make themselves feel superior.

Armed with the right information, steady practice, and concerted effort, you can reveal the confidence that already lies within you, be as pleasant and sociable as others may already think you are, and become as good a friend as you need to be to yourself.

I hope this book helps you on your path to understanding and beating your social anxiety. If you want more information, check out my comprehensive online treatment program, ebook, and podcast at overcomingsocialanxiety.com.

—Kyle MacDonald, author, *The Social Anxiety Survivor's Handbook*

A Note from the Author

When I was in the third grade, I came down with stomach flu right in the middle of a school day. I distinctly remember lying in the school's sickroom, the thin paper that covered the sickbed crinkling under my weight. The clock on the wall slowly ticked away the minutes as I waited for my father to pick me up. Above all, I remember the fear—the fear of not knowing what was happening to my body, the fear that my father might never show up, and the fear that I would vomit again with no control over when or how it happened.

This singular experience spawned years of anxiety, triggering a phobia disorder that controlled my daily life (although it would be a long time before I received my diagnosis). In college, a doctor finally confirmed that, yes, I struggled with an anxiety disorder. But, by that point, I had already guessed as much since most of my adolescence had been spent awake at night, trying to ease my anxious thoughts about any number of things. I knew I lived a life ruled by my anxious feelings, but it was still validating to have a medical professional give it a name.

Determined to not let anxiety rule my future, I began to study anxiety disorders while pursuing my first love: writing. I did what I believe everyone should do when they feel helpless: I educated myself. From that point on, I've continued to learn as much as I can about anxiety. I've continued to take baby steps every day in the pursuit of better mental health, despite setbacks and moments of frustration. I began sharing my own experiences and advice through my writing, which culminated in my dating and anxiety advice blog, The Anxious Girl's Guide to Dating. Along this path, one paved with the written word and the pursuit of understanding anxiety, I've arrived at *A Guide to Thriving with Social Anxiety*, which you now hold in your hands.

Although my personal experiences have directly affected my understanding and perspectives on living with anxiety, I have elected to leave my own stories out of the book. The focus of this book is on you, the reader, and helping you through your daily life. My hope is that the information, scenarios, and exercises within these pages will act as a guide while you strive to learn more about yourself and how anxiety influences your life. With this book, my goal is to serve as support and encouragement for your journey. I wish you growth, joy, and relief from anxiety.

With gratitude,
Hattie

PART I

A Fresh Start

Congratulations on making a fresh start on your journey toward a more fulfilling social and professional life. Since you're reading this book, you've likely been diagnosed with social anxiety disorder (SAD) by a health-care professional. If you haven't yet received a diagnosis, you can still read this book to familiarize yourself with the background and strategies; however, we recommend speaking with a doctor or therapist about your social anxiety to receive proper treatment and guidance.

Part I will provide background information about anxiety and SAD. We will define SAD from both a clinical perspective and a more subjective angle, and help you understand the differences between social anxiety and other anxiety disorders. Insight will be offered into what's happening in the brain and body of someone who experiences anxiety and how these factors can come together to interfere with daily life. Part I is also a road map for the rest of the book, describing how to put the practices and strategies provided throughout Part II to best use.

Even if you have been living with social anxiety for years and have turned to this book for the strategies covered in Part II to help you cope better in social settings, be sure to read Part I anyway. You might discover some new information or see something in a different light. One of the best ways to move toward better health and more enjoyment in life is to educate yourself. When you understand the reasons behind certain behaviors, you gain power over your situation and can make educated decisions on how best to move forward. Use this book as your companion as you explore new pathways toward greater comfort and confidence in all types of social situations.

What Is Social Anxiety?

At one time or another, everyone experiences feelings of nervousness or anxiety. For some, however, those feelings are all-pervading, impairing the ability to fully enjoy life. When it comes to social interaction, you might notice that your anxiety increases even during what should be enjoyable events, such as attending a friend's birthday party. In other cases, you might feel immobilized by anxiety over the prospect of going on a job interview, attending a meeting, or giving a presentation.

If you've picked up this book, you've made the choice to better understand this disorder and, in the process, to better understand yourself. Let's begin this journey of self-understanding with a scenario that might feel familiar to you.

QUICK QUIZ

You promised yourself you'd be more outgoing, so when a coworker invites you to attend a networking event with him, you force yourself to say yes. You already feel anxious about attending. You worry about looking foolish in front of your coworker, and you certainly don't want to seem too clingy. But then, to make matters worse, two days before the event, your coworker informs you that he can't make it after all; something came up. Immediately your mind is flooded with anxiety-inducing thoughts: You imagine walking into the event, without knowing a single person, and feeling uncomfortable with the idea of initiating or joining a conversation. You picture yourself standing in a corner all alone. You feel physically ill at the idea of going by yourself. Your heart is racing, your stomach is churning, and your palms are moist. Do you:

A. Understand your coworker's reason for being unable attend and, despite your anxiety-inducing thoughts, look forward to meeting some new, interesting people on your own?

B. Resent your coworker for getting you into this, and feel reluctant to go on our own, but still attend the event because you already paid for the ticket and hope to get something out of the experience?

C. Consider canceling completely, but then force yourself to go to the event for at least an hour because you know you'll be disappointed in yourself if you don't at least try?

D. Go to the event, but the entire time you're there, you obsessively pick apart everything you say and do, and wonder if anyone notices how nervous you are? You spend the majority of your time contemplating leaving. Then, once you're home, you spend the rest of the night going over everything you said and did. You wonder if anyone noticed that you tripped over your words or drew a blank, and you beat yourself up for not being more outgoing. You feel physically and emotionally exhausted.

A change in plans calls for a period of adjustment whether or not a person has social anxiety. Of course, it's comforting to have a companion in new or unfamiliar social situations; the difference is how you are affected by the prospect of facing a situation alone. How do you feel when a last-minute change of plans will affect you in an upcoming social situation? If you selected A, you're probably practicing your social coping skills with success. If you selected answers B or C, it's clear you're making an effort to overcome your social anxiety. If you selected D, you might be struggling with a level of social anxiety that disrupts your quality of life. Regardless of your choice in this particular scenario, read on to learn more about social anxiety and how to cope with it in a variety of social situations.

SAD: A Brief Walkthrough

You might already be familiar with the definition of social anxiety disorder, but for the purposes of this guide, let's take a look at it with fresh eyes. The following is the standard criteria for the classification of SAD as found in the *Diagnostic and Statistical Manual of Mental Disorders*, 5th Edition (DSM-5) (American Psychiatric Association):

A. Marked fear or anxiety about one or more social situations in which the individual is exposed to possible scrutiny by others. Examples include social interactions (e.g., eating or drinking), and performing in front of others (e.g., giving a speech).

B. The individual fears that he or she will act in a way or show anxiety symptoms that will be negatively evaluated (i.e., will be humiliating or embarrassing; will lead to rejection or offend others).

C. The social situations almost always provoke fear or anxiety.

D. The social situations are avoided or endured with intense fear or anxiety.

E. The fear or anxiety is out of proportion to the actual threat posed by the social situation and to the sociocultural context.

F. The fear, anxiety, or avoidance is persistent, typically lasting for 6 months or more.

G. The fear, anxiety, or avoidance causes clinically significant distress or impairment in social, occupational, or other important areas of functioning.

H. The fear, anxiety, or avoidance is not attributable to the physiological effects of a substance (e.g., a drug of abuse, a medication) or other medical condition.

I. The fear, anxiety, or avoidance is not better explained by the symptoms of another mental disorder, such as panic disorder, body dysmorphic disorder, or autism spectrum disorder.

J. If another medical condition (e.g., Parkinson's disease, obesity, disfigurement from burns or injury) is present, the fear, anxiety, or avoidance is clearly unrelated or is excessive.

According to the Anxiety and Depression Association of America (ADAA), anxiety disorders affect approximately 40 million adult Americans. Within this number, about 15 million suffer specifically from SAD, revealing that the condition is widespread and relatively common. It's important to keep in mind that everyone deals with anxiety from time to time; however, if you have an anxiety disorder

What Is a Panic Attack?

The ADAA describes a panic attack as the abrupt onset of intense fear or discomfort that reaches a peak within minutes and includes at least four of the following symptoms:

- Palpitations, pounding heart, or accelerated heart rate

- Sweating

- Trembling or shaking

- Sensations of shortness of breath or smothering

- Feelings of choking

- Chest pain or discomfort

- Nausea or abdominal distress

- Feeling dizzy, unsteady, light-headed, or faint

- Chills or heat sensations

- Paresthesia (numbness or tingling sensations)

- Derealization (feelings of unreality) or depersonalization (being detached from oneself)

- Fear of losing control or "going crazy"

- Fear of dying

If you experience panic attacks, know that a health-care professional can help you get your anxiety under control; this is a treatable condition.

that affects and interferes with your daily life, you are not alone. Support is available from a variety of sources. Remember, a consultation with a health-care professional is essential. Don't try to diagnose yourself.

A Brief History of the SAD Diagnosis

To better understand SAD and how treatment methods have evolved over the years, let's take a quick, but important, glimpse into the history of the diagnosis. While it's safe to assume that people were living with SAD before it appeared in a diagnostic manual, SAD (or social phobia, as it was referred to at the time) first appeared in the DSM-II in 1968, when social fears were defined as a specific phobia of social situations.

In 1980, when the DSM-III was released, social phobia became an individual psychiatric diagnosis. At this point, diagnostic criteria and procedures were still in the evolutionary stage, as individuals could not be diagnosed with both social phobia and a similar disorder termed avoidant personality disorder (APD). This complicated an accurate diagnosis, because APD—a disorder categorized by an intense feeling of inadequacy, sensitivity to what others think of them, and fears of casual conversations—shares a great deal in common with social phobia. This discrepancy changed in 1987 with revisions to the DSM-III, which further clarified the difference between the disorders. In 2013, with the publication of the DSM-5, the term *social phobia* was replaced by *social anxiety disorder* to reflect a broader understanding of the disorder.

Generalized anxiety disorder (GAD) was also introduced in the revised DSM-III in 1987. GAD shares some commonalities with SAD; however, it's important to be conscious of the distinctions between the two disorders to assess how best to move forward with treatment and growth.

GAD involves excessive anxiety and worry that aren't confined to a single feature. In a person with GAD, excessive anxiety and worry occur on more days than not for at least a six-month period in relation to a number of events or activities, not just social situations. Whereas SAD directly correlates to social-related situations, GAD is triggered by situations beyond social-specific activities, such as personal finances or the general safety of one's home. However, as mentioned previously, the two disorders do share common traits. For example, both SAD and GAD can leave a person feeling that his or her anxiety is difficult to control. People living with either disorder may experience an interruption of cognitive (mental) function, disturbed sleep patterns, and a loss of appetite. For those living with these disorders, the anxiety and worry interfere with daily life, both personally and professionally, making it difficult to execute everyday activities.

The commonalities between SAD and GAD speak to the chemical reactions going on in the brain of a person who experiences persistently high levels of anxiety. The levels of neurotransmitters and other chemicals in the brain can become imbalanced for a variety of reasons, thereby negatively affecting mood and behavior. Serotonin is the brain chemical that's most often associated with anxiety disorders. Acting as a neurotransmitter that relays information from one part of the brain to the other, serotonin is responsible for mood balance. If this neurotransmitter cannot reach its receptor sites in the brain or if the body produces insufficient amounts, a change in mood, anxiety, panic, or depression may result.

These biochemical factors are a primary reason why scientists are researching the connection between anxiety-related issues and genetics. While research has yet to identify a specific "anxiety" gene that passes the condition from one generation to the next,

Common Anxiety-Provoking Situations

When it comes to social anxiety, you might not experience the associated uncomfortable feelings and worrisome thoughts until you're faced with an anxiety-inducing situation. For people with social anxiety, the following situations are often difficult to approach with confidence and healthy anticipation:

- Going on an interview
- Attending a party
- Attending a networking event
- Starting a new job, school, or group activity
- Dating
- Speaking in public and/or giving a presentation
- Going out alone

observational studies have shown that anxiety disorders run in families. A predisposition for an anxiety disorder can be inherited, although individual symptoms of anxiety may manifest differently from those experienced by direct relatives. If one has a genetic predisposition for anxiety, environmental factors, such as a significant or traumatic life event, can trigger the disorder. If you have recently experienced a traumatic life event that has triggered your anxiety, contact a health-care professional who can provide you with understanding and support as you process the experience. Professionally trained *and* compassionate people are available to help you.

The Two Subtypes of SAD

There are two recognized subtypes of SAD. The first, the generalized subtype, is characterized by a fear of most social and/or performance situations. The second subtype, the nongeneralized subtype, is characterized by fears specifically related to public speaking and/or other performance activities.

The need for a distinction makes sense considering that many people who experience crippling fear at the thought of public speaking wouldn't consider themselves socially anxious otherwise. However, an overwhelming fear of public speaking can still interrupt your quality of life, especially if your profession requires it. You can seek help for this fear and benefit from the support of a trained professional who knows how to help you overcome it.

Regardless of how your particular case of social anxiety affects you or which subtype of SAD you most relate to, you can learn to successfully manage your symptoms with the right support, strategies, and treatment plan. However, an important initial step in learning to manage any health condition is understanding how your body reacts to certain factors and then using that information to assist you in developing your plan of action. The next chapter provides important insight.

CHAPTER

The Brain–Body Connection

Our thoughts have the ability to manifest as physical reactions in our bodies. The connection between our thoughts and physiological responses is clear—for example, feeling hungry after thinking about our favorite food, crying when recalling a particularly sad memory, or experiencing a racing heart when an exciting experience comes to mind. If you're living with social anxiety, it's important to pay attention to your thought patterns, precisely because they can exert such a powerful influence on your body. An awareness of your thoughts can help you start to gain control of what's going on in your mind and better manage your physical symptoms.

Thinking and Feeling

One of the most common traits of social anxiety is repetitive, unrelenting thoughts that take the form of debilitating worry. When faced with an anxiety-inducing situation, you might have various negative thoughts, such as the ones listed below, any of which can stop you from taking chances or enjoying new experiences. Do any of these thoughts sound familiar to you?

Common Thoughts Driven by Social Anxiety

- Everyone at the party will notice how anxious I feel.

- I've already canceled plans with this person twice, but I'm afraid if I meet up with her, I'll have a panic attack.

- What if I end up stuttering or stumbling over my words the way I did a few months ago?

- I know it's unreasonable to feel this nervous about meeting my new coworkers, but I can't stop worrying that my outfit is too formal . . . or maybe too casual.

- If I try to start a conversation, I'll end up saying something stupid.

Considering the connection between our brains and our bodies, it makes sense that negative thoughts, as well as unexpressed feelings (or pent-up emotions), can lead to uncomfortable physical manifestations. Anyone who has experienced a stressful situation will likely be able to recall the discomfort of a racing heart, a dry tongue, or difficulty swallowing.

Our bodies communicate with us all the time, sometimes before our minds even recognize danger. They are wired to perform the job of keeping us safe, and they take their cues from what's happening around us and inside us. However, for someone with social anxiety,

How the Body Responds to Fear and Anxiety

During an anxiety-inducing experience, the sympathetic nervous system typically triggers the fight-or-flight response, which results in the release of stress hormones into the bloodstream. These stress hormones create physical responses, such as accelerated heartbeat, headaches, nausea, sweating, muscle tension, and trembling. Over time, if the body routinely and excessively releases stress hormones, negative health consequences, such as a weakened immune system, chronic digestive disorders, short-term memory loss, and deteriorating cardiovascular function, may occur.

The flight-or-fight response is a normal response to fear. The associated physiological responses are intended to give us the ability to take action in dangerous situations. In other words, the fight-or-flight response is a life-saving reaction to threats in our natural environment—such as being stalked by a wild animal that wants to have us for dinner. Fortunately, in our modern world, this isn't something we normally experience. The problem arises from the fact that we generally don't need to feel fearful in most social situations, but when social anxiety is driving one's behavior, the body doesn't know the difference. In Chapter 6, you'll learn about exposure therapy, which is rooted in the idea that repeatedly facing a feared situation will gradually help you overcome the fear.

For now, just be aware that you don't need to be fearful in social situations. By becoming more aware of your physical reactions as they are related to your thoughts, you can make a conscious decision to get your fears in perspective and not allow them to dictate your life. Be proud of yourself for taking a step toward freedom from fear.

the body's reaction can result in daily physical disruptions. An anxious state can trigger numerous uncomfortable physical reactions, such as those listed below.

Common Physical Reactions Driven by Social Anxiety

- Increased heart rate
- Nausea and upset stomach
- Irritable bowel, including diarrhea
- Cognitive disruption, including confusion
- Muscle aches or tension
- Blushing
- Stuttering/stammering
- Shaking

The Difference Between Instinctual Fear and Anxiety

Fear is a natural response that motivates us to be alert. Animals often instinctually show fear when they are startled or exposed to a disturbance in their environment. After experiencing a particularly fear-inducing situation, animals will learn to be wary of that type of situation in the future. The fear has been triggered by a concrete experience or encounter. Once the immediate danger is past, the fear reaction often dissipates.

On the other hand, anxiety is often associated with imagined threats or actions, perhaps based on something that occurred in the past. Some studies speculate that anxiety is simply a more complex form of fear. The part of our brain that controls emotional behaviors, the amygdala, speedily incorporates information the rest of the cognitive processes, resulting in selective attention, explicit memory, and heightened perception. While the basis of the emotion may be linked to a prior experience that triggered genuine fear, the anxiety itself is often wrapped up in future potential threats (for example, worrying about possibly blushing during a business meeting). Fear is an immediate response to a threat, while anxiety is rooted in uncertainty and repetitive thoughts regarding a poor outcome. Therefore, it seems that anxiety is much more difficult to control than fear. Fortunately, you *can* learn to control it by becoming aware of the thoughts that are triggering your anxiety. (You'll learn more about this in Chapter 4.)

Ben, age 17, from San Francisco, California, noticed that he has been increasingly trying to avoid eating lunch in the school cafeteria. Ben has always been socially anxious, but a few months earlier, a specific event triggered a great deal of anxiety. He had entered the cafeteria, and on his way to his usual seat, one of the other students tripped him. He didn't fall, but his food tray splattered ketchup all over his shirt. When he regained his footing, someone exclaimed that he was blushing so much that his face was as red as the ketchup. A few people laughed at the joke. Ben was mortified. A lunch monitor witnessed the event, and the offender was sent to the principal's office. Later, he even apologized to Ben. But ever since this incident, Ben feels anxiety building up when he nears the cafeteria and hears the other students. Even though his school has a zero-tolerance policy toward bullying and the likelihood that a similar incident will happen again is slim, he still worries. If he had fallen, he could have hurt himself, but even worse, he had been embarrassed in front of his peers. He never wants to experience that again. He knows he should just get over it, but the more he

How Shyness and Introversion Differ from Social Anxiety

People living with SAD are often labeled as "shy" or "introverted." However, SAD isn't the same as either of those labels. Shyness is a general feeling of discomfort around people, usually when first meeting them or in large groups. The anxiety and discomfort associated with shyness may arise when a person first encounters an anxiety-inducing situation but then fades once he or she leaves the situation. An introverted person prefers to spend time alone following social interactions in order to recharge his or her energy. SAD, however, disrupts a person's everyday thoughts, patterns, and behaviors. This is a diagnosable condition, while shyness and introversion are personal characteristics. It's important not to minimize the experience of someone living with SAD by labeling him or her as "shy" or "introverted."

thinks about it, the more he feels himself wanting to avoid the cafeteria at lunchtime altogether.

In this example, you can see that Ben's anxiety stems from a specific incident that triggered authentic fear. Tripping and falling is a serious concern. However, as Ben contemplates going into the cafeteria, he is using his anxiety-inducing thoughts to convince him that he isn't safe and should avoid the situation entirely. Logically, he knows that going into the cafeteria isn't a threatening situation, but the shameful memories associated with the event reinforce for him that the cafeteria poses a danger.

Knowing how your body responds to what's going on in your mind is the first step to regaining control. So start by paying attention to your thoughts and feel how your body reacts to them. Really try to notice the connection. This awareness will help you practice the strategies in Part II. You're almost there. But first, the next chapter will help you get the most from this book.

CHAPTER

How to Use This Book

Let's return to the scenario in Chapter 1, in which you reluctantly decided to attend a networking event with a coworker who backed out of attending at the last minute. What is the advice you'd give someone facing this scenario? What would you do in this situation? Realistically, what might happen if you were to go to the event alone? If you had read and practiced the strategies in this book, you could have taken any number of steps to attend the networking event without experiencing debilitating anxiety. For example, you could have paused for a moment to become conscious of your negative thoughts and then reframed them to be more helpful and realistic. Having practiced mindfulness, you could have approached the event with confidence and simply allowed any perceived mistakes or flaws to pass by without judgment. You might have met new people and expanded your professional network.

Social anxiety makes people want to avoid situations that have the potential to lead to positive outcomes and social connections. Fortunately, social anxiety is a surmountable disorder. With the strategies in this book as part of your treatment plan, you can learn quick ways to manage your social anxiety and put your most confident self forward in any situation.

Picking and Choosing Strategies

Part II provides a variety of options for pursuing a more rewarding social and professional life. Consider all the strategies presented in the upcoming chapters carefully. It's important to discover what works best for you, so flip through the strategy chapters and give all the tips a try, when applicable, to uncover what's most helpful to you. You might be able to skip a step or two, or you might need to use all of them. These tools will help you in the moment, but to achieve your goals of enjoying yourself during social encounters and having a more fulfilling life, you must practice regularly and let these tools become part of your regular routine.

Setting Goals and Sticking to Them

Intent and action are two different things. Often it's easier to *intend* to do something than to actually follow through with action. This can be due to a variety of reasons (time restrictions, insecurities, financial limitations, or fear of failure, among others). Lack of follow through is a common setback for anyone starting off on a path toward change. Breaking old habits is difficult, which is why it's encouraged that you stick with a new behavior for at least 21 days before you can expect it to start becoming a habit. As

Celebrities and Social Anxiety

Some of the most famous celebrities struggle with SAD. Let's take a look at how they cope with it.

Adele This Grammy Award–winning singer has revealed she often experiences anxiety attacks before a live performance, sometimes even resulting in vomiting or wanting to flee the venue. In a two-part 2011 interview with MTV News, Adele explained that she calls to mind the strength she saw in other performers she looks up to—such as June Carter Cash and Beyoncé—to manage pre-performance anxiety.

Donny Osmond Although the Osmonds began performing very young, he wasn't immune to social anxiety and stage fright. When, as an adult, he found himself tempted to turn to alcohol to cope with his anxiety, he sought professional assistance and found relief in a combination of cognitive behavioral therapy (CBT) and medication.

Jennifer Lawrence The Hunger Games star has been open with the press regarding her struggles with anxiety during her childhood and teen years. She cites the stage and acting as helping her rediscover herself and her passion for life. Upon seeing Lawrence on stage, the actress's mother reportedly witnessed her daughter's anxieties disappear.

you approach the strategies in Part II, the main objective is to set yourself up for success, not failure. Be honest with yourself and establish realistic expectations up front so that you don't become discouraged and lose momentum:

- First, set up your intent for change. What is something you would like to work toward? What is outside your comfort zone, but still within reach? Spend some time truly defining what you'd like to accomplish and then write it down in a journal. You can use the journal pages provided in this book, your computer, or a notebook.

- In your journal, describe your goal and establish benchmarks for success. For example, if you're hoping to be more confident at work, how would that look? Perhaps you'd like to be able to have a casual conversation with at least two of your coworkers each day—write that down as a benchmark. You can even assign dates or deadlines for each step to help hold yourself accountable. During this process, you'll break down your goals and habits into easily attainable achievements, which will then help propel you forward.

- Another way to be held accountable is to enlist the help of a trusted friend or family member and share your plan with him or her. You can also seek out someone who hopes to achieve goals that are similar to yours and start a buddy system. Setting up a support system can help keep you on track.

- You also want to support yourself by preparing for any setbacks or roadblocks. Studies show that people who anticipate potential setbacks and make written plans for overcoming them persevere more and achieve higher levels of success than those who do not. If you're looking to strengthen your confidence on the job,

21 Days to Make a Habit

It's believed that doing something for 21 days straight will lead you right into the realm of habitude. This is one of the more important pieces of overcoming any anxiety disorder—creating new, healthier habits to replace your old ones. Maybe you're in the habit of starting the day off by listing every chore or task you have planned for the day. Instead, for the next 21 days, why not start your day by listing everything you are grateful for? Or, if you notice yourself holding your breath when you feel anxious, take that as a cue to practice deep-breathing exercises. Over time, if you're consistent and purposeful, your new habits will replace your old ones. For 21 days in a row, practice certain strategies listed in Part II, such as CBT techniques, mindfulness, or breathing exercises, and you'll eventually find yourself turning to those strategies without needing a reminder. Return to this book whenever you need a refresher or some positive reinforcement; you'll find time-based strategies for when you're on the go or in need of a quick reminder of what you can, and will, achieve.

first identify some situations that might make you feel discouraged. Perhaps a coworker criticizes a project that you worked tirelessly on. If that were to happen, how would you cope and continue to go after your goal?

- Like any new step you take toward managing your social anxiety, be sure to celebrate the small victories. This will remind you along the way that, yes, you're making strides toward your goal. Be proud of yourself for every move you make toward a more fulfilling life—even if it's simply the act of reading this book.

A Note about Medication

With this book in hand, you're on the path to further managing your social anxiety. You might be in the beginning stages, working with a therapist or clinician, trying to find out what your anxiety is all about, or seeking additional resources to augment your existing treatment plan. You might also be interested in learning about the medications that have the potential to help you cope better with SAD. Detailed information regarding medication goes beyond the scope of this book, as this is a sensitive topic. Many factors should be taken into account, so it's essential that this discussion occur between the person seeking treatment for SAD and a clinician licensed to prescribe medication. Most medical professionals do recommend using medication in tandem with alternative treatments, such as exercise, diet, or CBT, but each individual has unique needs. Speak with a health-care professional to explore the best options for you.

Common Medications Prescribed to Treat SAD

SSRIS Selective serotonin reuptake inhibitors (SSRIs) block the reuptake, or reabsorption, of serotonin. Mood is improved with the increase in available serotonin. Examples of SSRIs include fluoxetine (Prozac), paroxetine (Paxil), sertraline (Zoloft), citalopram (Celexa), and escitalopram (Lexapro). Side effects of SSRIs may include insomnia, sexual dysfunction, and weight gain.

SNRIS Serotonin and norepinephrine reuptake inhibitors (SNRIs) act in the same way as SSRIs; however, they increase serotonin and norepinephrine (another neurotransmitter). Examples of SNRIs include venlafaxine (Effexor), duloxetine (Cymbalta), and mirtazapine (Remeron). Side effects of SNRIs may include upset stomach, sexual dysfunction, and insomnia.

BENZODIAZEPINES These medications are generally used for short-term anxiety management as they are primarily used for reduction in muscular tension and therefore support relaxation. Examples of benzodiazepines include lorazepam (Ativan), alprazolam (Xanax), and diazepam (Valium). Side effects of benzodiazepines may include lowered effectiveness over long-term use and may also cause upset stomach, dizziness, depression, and memory loss.

It's rare that any given medication will work on the first try for an anxiety-related disorder. Oftentimes, the effects of a medication can take up to three weeks to appear. This will most likely result in several trial-and-error periods with the support of your health-care professional to find the right balance. Before treatment, it's also important to inform your health-care professional of any and all medications, including over-the-counter and natural remedies you're taking in order to avoid any complications due to drug interactions.

You'll have to work closely with your health-care professional to determine what will work best for you in terms of type of medication and the proper dosage. It's important to be honest and open about any side effects you experience. This will guarantee the best possible outcome as you seek relief from SAD. This can be a frustrating, time-consuming process, but if you're seeking relief through medication, it's worthwhile to stick with it.

In Part II, you'll learn about various strategies you can use to complement any medical approaches you may be exploring. With this refresher course on social anxiety under your belt, you're now ready to take action and start practicing the anxiety-relieving strategies presented in the upcoming chapters. Keep in mind what you learned in this chapter as you begin your journey of exploration, and always remember to follow up intent with action.

PART II

The Strategies

I n this part, you'll learn about nonmedical strategies that can help you manage your social anxiety, including quick exercises you can practice on the spot. As mentioned previously, be open to discussing the topic of medication with your doctor or therapist; together, you can find a combination of strategies that work best in your particular case. In the meantime, use this part of the book to familiarize yourself with complementary avenues for managing your anxiety, including CBT, exposure therapy, mindfulness, meditation, and breathing exercises, as well as nutrition, exercise, and natural remedies. You'll also learn how to develop your confidence, assertiveness, and appreciation for life.

Over time, you'll likely discover that a combination of strategies works best for you, bearing in mind that this will be a process of testing different strategies and learning in what ways they helped, or did not help. As you work through this book, don't be afraid to stumble along the way; persevere and maintain the belief that you're worth the effort. It's what growth is all about—we can't grow without the occasional stumble, and when you stumble, you can and should view your missteps as a reminder that you're trying something new. Renew your intentions and remain committed. With hard work, patience, and time, you will be all the more closer to achieving a happy and healthy life.

Cognitive Behavioral Therapy (CBT)

CBT is possibly the most popular strategy for treating social anxiety. This form of therapy is most effective for anyone who has thoughts or beliefs that cause life-disrupting behaviors that interfere with interpersonal relationships, professional life, and internal self-worth. For this reason and more, CBT can be highly effective in helping people with social anxiety regain control over their thought patterns—as well as their lives.

Do you often feel controlled by your thought patterns? If so, CBT can help you take back some of that control. This chapter offers information about this therapy as well as quick tips for applying

CBT techniques in everyday situations. Even if you only have five minutes to get your anxiety under control, this chapter will give you strategies to reorient your thoughts and behaviors on the spot. While you can practice many CBT techniques on your own, you may want to consider seeking the help of a therapist who can guide you through the process and offer additional insight. In the meantime, consider the scenarios and thought patterns discussed in this chapter to learn how CBT can help you find relief from your anxiety-related negative thoughts.

A Note on Psychotherapy

If you're considering entering into ongoing therapy for your social anxiety, keep in mind that therapy isn't a one-size-fits-all approach. There are different methods of therapy, including the psychodynamic approach (aka "the talking cure"), CBT, interpersonal therapy (IPT), and others. Every mental health professional has his or her own preferred style and philosophy. While the choices of therapeutic approaches can seem daunting at first, give yourself permission to try different forms of therapy until you find one to meet your needs. What's most important is finding a supportive environment in which you feel you can speak openly about your experiences.

Therapy is a collaborative experience, and it's okay to "interview" health-care professionals until you find one who feels like a good match. If you find yourself in a state of discomfort with a particular therapist, you might feel uncomfortable speaking candidly, which can then inhibit your pursuit of a more fulfilling life. Allow yourself the space and time to find someone who provides you with a certain level of personal comfort. There's more about this in the Conclusion.

QUICK QUIZ

You're about to meet a new acquaintance for lunch, and although you wish you could just look forward to the time you'll spend with her, a recurring thought keeps popping into your mind: *She probably doesn't really like me. She's just having lunch with me out of pity.* Do you:

A. Tell yourself that's probably true and plan a strategy to get out of the lunch date?

B. Consider it to be true, but because you're incredibly hungry, you decide to suffer through the bad feelings while you eat?

C. Transfer your negative feelings about the situation to negative feelings about your acquaintance and seethe at her throughout the meal?

D. Acknowledge the negative thought, but realize it's coming from an anxious place, and try to replace it with a positive thought such as, *It's great that I have a chance to engage with someone new!*

If you selected A, B, or C, you're probably looking for new ways to approach situations with a more positive approach. If you selected D, you're likely already employing CBT techniques, maybe without realizing it. Regardless of your answer to this quiz, or even if you aren't quite sure what you'd do in this scenario, continue reading to learn more about CBT and how it can help you turn negatives into positives.

What Is CBT All About?

CBT is centered on becoming aware of our thoughts, better under-standing them, and changing our thinking patterns and behaviors. It's rooted in the idea that our thoughts, not external circumstances or people, cause our behaviors. People living with social anxiety tend to have habitually negative or false beliefs. With a therapist's guidance, or even when applying CBT techniques on your own, you can take the initiative to begin identifying the unhealthy thought patterns that can result in self-destructive behaviors. Through CBT, you can begin to identify these thoughts, test them in real-life scenarios, and start replacing them with more constructive, posi-tive thoughts.

Dr. Aaron T. Beck developed the cognitive therapy approach in the 1960s following his research on people with depression. During the study, he discovered that participants had negative thought patterns that appeared almost automatically. These "automatic thoughts" often fell into one of three categories: negative thoughts about themselves, negative thoughts about the world, and negative thoughts about the future. Beck wondered if helping to change the thinking patterns in these people would change their outlooks on life, and thereby have a positive effect on their behaviors. Based on his findings, Beck spearheaded the CBT approach to psychotherapy, which focused on helping clients identify negative thoughts and evaluate their validity objectively and realistically.

Many of the "internal scripts" that play repeatedly in the minds of those living with social anxiety are negative. Let's revisit the scenario in which a new acquaintance invites you to lunch. In the scenario, you automatically thought the person invited you out of pity and actually dislikes you. Using CBT techniques, you could look at this thought objectively. This immediate, almost instinctual, negative reaction is not likely based in reality. The situation (meeting a new person for lunch) triggered a negative thought pattern, and CBT can help you recognize this automatic response, become aware of the thoughts, test whether the thoughts have any validity, and then create a healthier, more realistic script for a similar situation. In other words, you can tell yourself that it's likely your new acquaintance neither pities you nor dislikes you, but actually invited you to lunch simply to get to know you better.

Everyone is capable of developing new thought patterns and habits. Although it often takes commitment and time, CBT is an excellent place to start if you'd like to develop a more positive internal voice by examining negative core beliefs in a more objective light. (Negative core beliefs are discussed in more detail later in this chapter.) Are you worried that you don't have what it takes? Know this: you absolutely *do* have what it takes. Read on to find out why.

CBT in Practice

If you're feeling personally motivated and capable of objectively observing your own thoughts, then you're capable of practicing CBT techniques. It's easy to feel intimidated by something with such an official-sounding name, but be assured that you already have the skills to practice it. You *are* capable of practicing and mastering the healing qualities of CBT. Answer the following questions to discover this for yourself:

- Can you pay attention to your thoughts?
- Can you identify which thoughts are negative and which are positive?
- Can you start testing those thoughts by asking yourself if they are realistic?

If You Only Have 5 Minutes

CHECK IT, CATCH IT, CHANGE IT

This basic exercise sums up CBT in a nutshell. If you have a negative thought, don't try to brush it off or minimize it. Allow it in, and take stock of the thought. Acknowledge why you feel that way. Then plan to build on this information for a positive outcome. Here's how:

1. If you feel yourself becoming anxious, pause for a moment and turn your attention to the thoughts in your mind.

2. Try to identity one specific thought that feels particularly unhelpful to you in this situation. For example, if you're about to return an item of clothing at the store, identity a single thought such as, *The clerk will think I'm an idiot for not having a receipt and won't allow me to return the item.*

3. Next, identify the type of scenario this is: You're required to speak to someone you don't know and ask that person for help returning an item. Remind yourself that an unhelpful sales associate could be preoccupied by something going on in his or her own life, and the person's behavior isn't necessarily a reflection of what he or she thinks of you or your intelligence level.

4. Replace your current negative thought with a more helpful, positive thought. For example, *This person is in the business of customer service and is here to help me. Even without a receipt, I can still return the item without one. If not, that's okay, too, and it doesn't reflect my level of intelligence.*

Throughout your day, perform quick check-ins to create a habit out of changing a negative, unhelpful thought to a positive, helpful one. If you keep at it, this practice will become second nature to you.

- Can you construct a thought that would be more helpful to you in the moment?

Yes. You can do all of these things. All you need to do is slow down, listen closely to your mind and body, and make conscious choices based on your observations. Not sure where to start? Try the following five-minute exercise.

Common Types of Anxious Thinking

As Beck discovered in his study on depression, people tend to have negative thoughts in three different categories: negative thoughts about themselves, negative thoughts about the world, and negative thoughts about the future. Over time, research has fine-tuned the various thoughts a socially anxious person has that may fall into one, or several, of these categories. As you look through these examples of common negative thoughts in a socially anxious person, see if any feel familiar to you. Have you had similar thoughts about a situation at one time or another? Have you noticed yourself believing similar things about yourself?

Keep a pen handy and take some notes on negative thought patterns that feel familiar to you and your experiences. You can use a journal for this purpose. Having these notes handy will be helpful later for tracking your progress or gaining further insight during future journaling exercises.

Probability Overestimation

Probability overestimation is allowing your fears to dictate your thoughts and behaviors while overriding rational probability. For example, if your sister asks if she can set you up on a blind date with her coworker, you may feel convinced that this person is a criminal who will kidnap you despite the fact that your sister has known the person for years and the odds of being kidnapped are low. Can you think of a time when you've reacted to something by engaging in probability overestimation? How did this feel? How might you replace this reaction with a more positive thought?

Mind Reading

Mind reading is assuming that you know what another person is thinking about you. Usually, these assumptions are negative and reflect insecurities you may hold about yourself. For example, when you walk into a business meeting, you might immediately start thinking, *That person can't stop staring at the zit on my chin. She thinks I'm disgusting. She's wondering why I even came to this meeting.* Are there times when you find yourself magically trying to read the thoughts of those around you? Are these thoughts usually helpful or unhelpful? Can you ever actually know what others are thinking without their actually telling you what's on their mind?

Personalization

Personalization is assuming responsibility for a situation that isn't your responsibility or within your control. Even if a situation includes numerous other responsible parties, you often feel the whole burden of the results. For example, let's say you attend a dinner party and bring a broccoli and cheese casserole to contribute to the buffet-style meal. If you overhear someone complaining about being lactose intolerant and not being able to eat any of the food, you might immediately think, *This is all my fault . . . I could've made something else. Why did I bring something with cheese in it?* Can you think of a time when you've felt the full weight of a situation that wasn't entirely your responsibility? How have you reacted in such a moment? How can you help yourself see that others share the responsibility?

"Should" Statements

"Should statements" arise when you feel that something *should* go or be a certain way. These types of thoughts occur when you're feeling inadequate or insecure about your social skills and thinking along the lines of *I should be better at making eye contact with strangers.* It's a familiar thought pattern that surfaces after leaving a situation in which you felt distressed. You may repeatedly go over things you said or did and tell yourself, *When I said that, I really embarrassed myself. I should have said this instead.* Do you have a habit of telling yourself what you "should" be doing or how a situation "should" go? How do these moments make you feel? How can you rephrase them to be more helpful in those moments?

Catastrophic Thinking

Catastrophic thinking, or *catastrophizing,* is believing that the worst-case scenario will actually happen. This thought pattern is familiar to any of us who remember our teenage years, when everything felt like a life-altering scenario. But for those with social anxiety, thoughts like, *All my friends will hate me if I wear the wrong clothes,* can appear on a daily basis, making them fear taking even the slightest chance. For example, you might imagine worst-case scenarios, such as a crowd of people laughing at you or a date telling you he or she would rather die than go out with you again. Do you find yourself imagining worst-case scenarios in life? How have you reacted to these situations in the past and how would you prefer to react?

All-or-Nothing Thinking

All-or-nothing thinking is believing that if something you want to happen doesn't happen, then it never will. For someone living with social anxiety, these all-or-nothing thoughts can be frequent, unhelpful, and paralyzing. You might be terrified to give a presentation at work because you're thinking, *If I mess up during this presentation now, I'll never get a promotion.* What are some situations that trigger your all-or-nothing thinking? How do you usually react when these thoughts occur?

Selective Attention and Memory

Selective attention and memory means choosing to pay more attention to certain kinds of information and memories. For example, let's say your boss gives you an annual performance review. You might walk away only remembering her say that you need to show more confidence and forgetting how she applauded you for having excellent organizational skills. This type of thought pattern usually comes in the form of you seeking information that reinforces your insecurities and fears. Do you find yourself focusing on only the negatives expressed to you, even if the positive feedback far outweighed it?

Negative Core Beliefs

Negative core beliefs are fundamentally held beliefs about yourself that spark your other anxious thought patterns and behaviors. For example, perhaps you have a negative core belief about yourself that you aren't worthy of success. You may come across a help-wanted advertisement for a job you think you'd be great at, but you don't even apply for the job. Or, if you do end up applying and getting an interview, your belief that you aren't worthy of success might show up as a lack of self-confidence during the interview. In other words, your actions and behaviors are reflecting your negative core belief. Identifying these negative core beliefs—the roots of many of your anxious thoughts and behaviors—may take time and perseverance, but it's well worth it in the end. Can you identify some of your negative core beliefs? How do they influence your thoughts and behaviors?

Using CBT to Counteract Anxious Thinking

CBT embraces the idea that you can start identifying when you're having an anxiety-inducing thought, the form that thought is taking, whether or not that thought is helpful, and how you can restructure that thought to become helpful.

You have the strength and power to make a difference in your thought patterns by developing these habits. It's important to remember that you are never helpless. But, as you've learned, a habit doesn't form overnight. It will take a commitment from you to develop more positive thought patterns. If you can make a conscious effort every day to counteract your anxious thinking with CBT, you're off to a strong start. Consider this example of someone who would benefit from making this commitment:

Lisa, age 51, from Salem, Oregon, works as an office assistant at a middle school. She has struggled with social anxiety her entire life, and, despite loving the school she works for, she finds parts of her job very stressful. For example, every morning she fields phone calls from parents who call to report a student's absence. Oftentimes,

(10) If You Only Have 10 Minutes
ADDRESS YOUR CONCERNS

You're about to give a big presentation at work. The idea of public speaking makes you nervous in general, but your present concern is that your coworkers will focus on the flaws in your presentation rather than on how valuable your information is or how much hard work you put into the preparation. Follow these steps to discover how you can turn this concern around for a more positive outcome:

1. At your desk or in a quiet place, write down all your fear-provoking concerns and what you anticipate the negative responses might be to your presentation.

2. Directly address each of your concerns. For example, if your concern is that the presentation doesn't give enough detail on a certain topic, you can address this with the thought, *That's all right. That topic will be covered at next week's meeting.* If your concern is that certain material might be confusing, you can think, *I'm well prepared for this presentation, so if anyone is confused, I can clearly explain it.*

3. Acknowledge that it's okay to be aware of the areas in yourself and your work that might need improvement. Remind yourself that everyone is still learning and growing. Giving this presentation will help you grow in experience.

Sometimes simply being aware of your own failings—after carefully considering them objectively—before you walk into a situation can improve your mood and confidence. So whether it's giving a presentation at work, going on a first date, or asking a gas station attendant for directions, remind yourself that you aren't perfect and that's perfectly okay.

these parents are hurried and stressed, and sometimes they are rude to Lisa. Their rudeness leaves her feeling very anxious.

Every morning, Lisa arrives at work with tense shoulders, a queasy stomach, and sweaty palms, knowing she'll have to answer the phone and speak with parents. She drives the same route to work every day and repeatedly thinks, *I should be better at talking on the phone. I should be used to it by now. I should know how to stand up for myself if someone is rude to me. I shouldn't be so weak.*

If Lisa were practicing CBT techniques, she would be able to pause and identify her thoughts as "should" statements. She would be able to acknowledge that just the act of driving to work triggers these thoughts and recognize that they are unhelpful. She would also be able to identify the manner in which her body reacts to these thoughts. Perhaps Lisa could take a new route to work and observe what she sees on the way there. During the drive, she could practice new thought patterns such as: *I don't encounter unfriendly parents every morning. There is no way to know if I'll encounter one today. What I do know is that I'm competent at my job and always do my best work. I'm thankful to be employed at a school I care about.*

It often helps to pause and feel grateful for what you *do* have rather than fixate on what you *should* have. If Lisa committed to restructuring her thought patterns on a daily basis, it would eventually turn into a habit and feel more natural.

Breaking Your Thoughts into Smaller Parts

CBT aims to make your anxiety feel more manageable by breaking your thoughts down into smaller parts. For example, if you have a negative core belief that's emotionally charged, such as "I'm unlovable," your thought might be something like, *No one wants to be my friend because I'm anxious, and I have nothing of interest to talk about.* Or you might be thinking, *I'll never find a life partner because my personality is so flat*. With CBT, you can look at these thoughts and get to the "core" of the matter by figuring out what is underlying them. In both of these cases, your negative core belief might be that you are unlovable.

When you recognize this, you can then begin to reframe the negative core belief by reminding yourself that you are lovable. There is a lot about you that is positive, even if you're suffering from anxiety and worrisome thoughts. Practicing CBT techniques can help you begin identifying when this negative core belief is triggered, why it's triggered, and the type of thoughts that arise from this belief. By understanding the way this belief manifests in your thinking habits, you can slowly begin to adjust your thoughts and behaviors to eventually adjust this core belief. Know that it takes time, but it's time well spent.

CBT can be a powerful tool to help you overcome your anxiety-inducing thought patterns. Examining your thoughts gives you the important opportunity to redirect your mind toward helpful thoughts that will bring you closer to your goal. Like anything, this approach takes consistent practice. Keep it up, and you'll keep discovering new ways to turn your thoughts around.

If You Have 30 Minutes

TRACK YOUR THOUGHT PATTERNS

Keeping a journal is a great way to gauge your progress toward achieving your goal. It can also help you begin to identify your negative core beliefs, which are often the root of many anxious thoughts and behaviors. If you're able to set aside 30 minutes every day (or at least from time to time) to track your thoughts, you'll likely start noticing patterns that you didn't realize were there. To experience these benefits, take the following steps:

1. At the end of the day, write down what you struggled with the most. Specify the time of day it occurred and try your best to identify what triggered the situation. How did you deal with it? What do you expect for the next day?

2. Try to identify any specific thoughts you had during these moments and see if they match any of the common types of anxious thinking explored earlier in this chapter.

3. Honestly assess how you dealt with the situation.

4. Try to thoroughly outline how you'll react the next time you encounter a similar situation. Try to visualize how you want to think and act in a similar moment that will feel healthy and helpful to you and your growth.

Living with social anxiety can make you feel disconnected from your thoughts and body. Sitting down and putting pen to paper, or fingers to keyboard, will remind you that you can choose to better understand yourself and create positive change with that awareness.

Mindfulness

As you are becoming more aware of your thought patterns and habits with the assistance of CBT techniques, it's also important to take a moment from time to time to be fully present—in other words, to be mindful. Mindfulness plays a vital role in helping alleviate stress and anxiety. Whereas CBT focuses on identifying and changing your thought processes, mindfulness focuses on finding acceptance and peace with your thoughts. CBT is more about action, while mindfulness is more about inaction, so to speak.

For example, imagine being outside on a summer day, gently observing the clouds as they pass through the blue sky. Your attention may not linger on any one cloud for too long, but instead you simply notice it and allow it to drift from your focus. This is how mindfulness works. You are present in a moment. You notice your thoughts and feelings as they drift past, but you notice them without judgment. While this may seem like a difficult task for someone living with social anxiety, the more you practice it, the more natural it will feel. This chapter will help you explore how to sharpen your mindfulness skills and learn to live with more awareness of the moment you are in right now.

QUICK QUIZ

You wake up in the morning, and your first thought is that you need to start a load of laundry before you get ready for work. But you suddenly remember that your washing machine is broken. You start to worry that you can't afford to fix it, and you aren't even sure if you'll have time to call a repairperson. Even the idea of calling a repairperson makes your heart race. Anyway, your schedule is jam-packed, and to top it off you're supposed to give a coworker you barely know a ride to the airport after work. What will you talk about? Do you:

A. Allow your thoughts to run wild, listing everything you have to do for the day and worrying that you won't be able to handle it all?

B. Allow yourself to worry about your day for several minutes, but then get up and get started on the first task?

C. Take out a piece of paper and create a to-do list for the day, even before getting out of bed?

D. Quietly observe your thoughts for several minutes without judgment before reminding yourself that you only need to take your day one task at a time?

If you selected D, you already have some of the basic building blocks of mindfulness. If you selected A, B, or C, this chapter will help you better understand how you can become more accepting and compassionate toward your thought processes so that they

5 If You Only Have 5 Minutes

SIT, BE SILENT, AND BE PRESENT

We often find ourselves automatically performing the tasks of our daily routines without thinking twice. We aren't just going through the motions; we are *running* through them. We face demands from every angle—our jobs, families, friends, and ourselves. Then, all too often, the voice inside our head demands even more of us. This can be true for everyone, not just for people with social anxiety; however, in the case of an anxiety disorder, the effects can feel magnified. Be assured that, if you take time to slow down and silence that voice for just a few minutes, you *can* regain a sense of peace. A few minutes of mindfulness can transform your whole day. Here's how to practice:

1. Sit in a quiet space where you feel comfortable. Don't look at your phone, don't spend too much time considering passersby, and don't speak. In other words, don't do anything but sit quietly. This is your opportunity to be in your body.

2. If a worrisome thought enters your mind, quietly observe it from a distance. Allow it to pass by without trying to grasp at it.

3. Perform a quick body scan, noticing any tension in the muscles of your face, neck, back, or elsewhere. Notice your breath, and try to tune in to the beat of your heart.

4. When the five minutes are up, thank yourself for taking this time out of your day to be mindful and focus on your well-being.

Sometimes the day may feel so full that you think you don't have even five minutes to be mindful. However, if you choose to prioritize your health and achieve your goal to effectively manage your social anxiety, you *will* find five minutes. Give yourself permission to sit, be silent, and be present.

do not dictate your actions. Mindfulness often comes in handy for those living with social anxiety by helping them reorient the tone of a situation—for example, by replacing the stressful morning to-do list with calm gratitude for another day of possibilities. By practicing the suggestions in this chapter, you can start observing your thoughts and your present state without judgment, rather than allowing your thoughts to dictate the tone of your day.

What Is Mindfulness?

Mindfulness is focused awareness and acceptance of the present moment. As a practice, mindfulness is derived from ancient Buddhist meditation practices and draws from other Eastern philosophies as well. This practice gained traction in the United States primarily through the work of Jon Kabat-Zinn, who developed the Mindfulness-Based Stress Reduction (MBSR) program in 1979 at the University of Massachusetts Medical School. Throughout the 80s and to the present day, research on mindfulness has offered us a good understanding of the health benefits of a mindfulness practice, which are discussed in the next section.

Although mindfulness shares many of the same qualities as meditation, it's not quite the same thing. Meditation is the practice of quieting the mind and, in a way, shutting out the outside world. (Meditation is explored in greater depth in Chapter 7.) Meanwhile, mindfulness encourages us to be conscious of our surroundings by being fully present in the moment.

Pay attention to where your mind is at this moment. Hopefully, it's focused on the words on this page. But what else is going on in your mind? What do you usually focus on? Chances are you often find yourself thinking about the past or worrying about the future. You might notice that you spend a lot of time planning ahead or feeling upset over something that did or didn't happen. Focusing your thoughts on the past or future pulls your attention away from being in the present moment. In the present moment, you can focus on what is. For example, if you focus without judgment on how you're feeling right now and simply accept those feelings as part of your experience, you can start developing more self-compassion. This, in turn, will allow you to extend your compassion to your family, friends, and strangers alike.

As Jon Kabat-Zinn points out in the short video *What Is Mindfulness?*, which was part of a larger talk presented by the Greater Good Science Center (GGSC) at the University of California, Berkeley, the Chinese character for *mindfulness* combines the ideograms for "presence" and "heart." If you find yourself losing focus on the purpose of mindfulness, bring yourself back to the concept of "presence of heart." By bringing awareness to your heart, you can embrace the importance of appreciating the moment in which you are living.

The Benefits of Practicing Mindfulness

Over the last few decades, countless studies have uncovered the benefits of practicing mindfulness. Studies show that one of the reasons mindfulness is so beneficial to those living with social anxiety is that it reduces the number of negative thoughts and increases the number of positive thoughts an individual experiences. Mindfulness encourages us to slow down and take time to be conscious of our actions. It reminds us to be present in the moment and to not only notice everything around us and everything we touch, but also to be purposeful in our actions.

The GGSC has been studying mindfulness and the various ways in which it benefits our health for years. GGSC has collected a good deal of data supporting the benefits of mindfulness, which is available for review on its website (see the resources section). For example, various studies cited have shown that practicing mindfulness can help strengthen the immune system, increase positive emotions, improve memory and attention skills, cultivate compassion, alleviate symptoms of post-traumatic stress disorder (PTSD) in veterans, and help relieve the stress associated with professional occupations such as health-care worker and educator.

You can practice mindfulness any time of the day. All it takes is pausing briefly to be present in that moment.

Breaking the Stress–Anxiety Cycle Under Pressure

Oftentimes, stress creates anxiety, and, in turn, anxiety creates stress. This can turn into a self-sustaining cycle that threatens to control your actions. For example, say you're running late for a dinner reservation with a friend, and you feel the stress starting to build; your symptoms are a racing heart and fuzzy thinking. This stress may then trigger anxiety over having dinner with your friend. You might say to yourself, *He's going to be angry with me for showing up late.* The more anxious you become, the more stressed you feel. These feelings feed off one another in an endless loop.

Try this instead: You're running late. Okay. Pause for a few minutes and focus your attention on the present moment. What sounds do you hear? Are any smells present? How does the texture of your shirt feel against your skin? Instead of judging the situation and worrying about what should be happening or how you're coming up short, instead observe your feelings and thoughts with compassion. Allowing yourself to "just be" helps release the pressure, and you can be calm as you experience the rest of the day.

10 If You Only Have 10 Minutes

PAUSE TO REVIEW AND REFLECT

After an anxiety-inducing event (or even just a taxing day), take a little while to mentally review the day's events while recalling your feelings during the process. It's important to take time for introspection, because it allows you to process your thoughts and feelings and reconnect with your inner self. Take these steps:

1. Find a quiet, comfortable place to sit and reflect on your day.

2. Review the events that might have caused your feelings of distress and anxiety. Try to identify the point at which any uncomfortable feelings first arose.

3. Quickly scan your body to identify whether you still feel residual physiological effects of this event. Without judgment, observe where in your body you feel anxious or tense.

4. Imagine the event(s) from the day as if they are drifting past you in the sky, like a cloud—merely an object for you to observe from a distance.

Taking just 10 minutes at the end of your day to practice being present in your thoughts and feelings will help you start making a habit out of mindfulness. You'll develop the skills to evaluate, without judgment or more anxiety, the thoughts you have about an anxiety-inducing day.

Practicing Mindfulness When Dealing with Social Anxiety

Some people might find mindfulness difficult to practice, especially those with anxious, hyperactive minds. When faced with an anxiety-inducing situation, it can be easy to forget to take time to be calm and remain in the moment. Whether you're hoping to go to a party or contemplating trying a new dance class at the community center, your anxious thoughts will often try to convince you not to take a chance. In that moment, try to simply observe these unhelpful thoughts and let them pass.

It's okay to feel challenged by the practice of mindfulness. When you feel challenged, it means you're trying something new that's triggering your growth. When practicing mindfulness while also dealing with social anxiety, remember to be compassionate with yourself during the process. It's easy to feel frustrated when you can't stay present and observe what's going on in your mind or body without getting caught up in it. When you have a hard time being present in the moment, it's easy to think, *I can't do this*. Remind yourself that it takes time and practice. Nobody perfects mindfulness on the first try—or the second.

The Tibetan lama Mingyur Rinpoche, who struggled with anxiety as a child, likens mindfulness to watching snow fall on a warm rock. As thoughts or feelings enter your mind, observe them as you would snow falling. Imagine that they hit a warm rock, immediately melting and disappearing into the stone. It doesn't mean your thoughts weren't present and didn't take form. However, the more you practice observing your thoughts, the more you'll realize they all melt away with time to be replaced by new thoughts.

Being Mindful of Your Own Needs

It's not uncommon for people to spend their days taking care of others' needs and worrying about everything they still have to do. For example, maybe your children need to be chauffeured to after-school practice, your family needs help around the house, your boss asks you to meet just one more deadline, or your neighbor needs another favor. It's easy to spend an entire day without being mindful of your own needs. While it's selfless and admirable to be of service to the people around you, it's equally important to be of service to yourself. Why don't you take more time for yourself during the day? Why don't you engage in behaviors just for you and simply enjoy being in the present moment? Is it because you feel guilty, as if you aren't entitled to stop what you're doing or thinking about to just appreciate the ordinary moments of a day? Consider this example:

Charlotte, age 42, from Olympia, Washington, visits her ailing father every day during the week to help with household chores and cook meals. She also brings her children to gymnastics practice twice a week and helps them with their homework. Her husband has picked up a second job to help cover the bills and feels bad that he can't help out more around the house. Charlotte struggled with social anxiety a lot in her twenties and has recently started noticing some of the symptoms returning with intensity. She knows that she needs to slow down and allow herself to simply be in the moment. However, Charlotte feels guilty whenever she contemplates taking a little time for herself every day to just be present. She knows people depend on her, and she feels selfish for wanting downtime. She worries that her family will think she doesn't love them if she doesn't keep going, planning, and doing things for them.

If You Have 30 Minutes

BE MINDFUL DURING A DAILY ROUTINE

This exercise is an opportunity for you to try it another way, which can also help ease any anxious feelings you might be having. Just follow these steps:

1. Choose an activity you tend to perform automatically—for example, your morning routine. Let's say you wake up every morning and take a shower. Then you brush your teeth, comb your hair, and make a cup of coffee. Make an intention to practice mindfulness during this morning routine.

2. As you go about your routine, carefully take note of the physical and emotional sensations you experience. Notice the water as it hits your skin. How does this make you feel? What sensation does your tongue experience when the toothpaste foams in your mouth? How does it taste, smell, and feel?

3. As you observe each action, be grateful for each moment. Not everyone on this earth has access to showers, toothbrushes, combs, and the like. As you're being present to the experiences and how they feel, take a moment to also feel gratitude.

When you choose to be present during an activity that you usually perform on autopilot, it forces you to truly be engaged in the moment, experiencing every minute detail. This, in turn, quiets potentially negative or stress-inducing thoughts that could try to enter your mind.

From an objective perspective, it seems only fair that Charlotte should take some time for herself throughout the day. However, the guilt she feels prohibits her from taking the time she needs to simply appreciate her life. It's possible that Charlotte is struggling to value herself as much as she values the other people in her life. It's possible that she's more concerned with her future tasks than being present for whatever is right in front of her.

Do you identify with Charlotte's dilemma? Pay attention to how you feel when you want to take a break. Do you feel guilty? If so, why do you think you feel guilty? Make an effort to communicate with others that your desire for some downtime doesn't reflect your feelings for them. Remember that before you can take care of others, you need to take care of yourself. So, be mindful of your needs and spend some time just being present.

Mindfulness isn't a difficult state to achieve as long as you give yourself permission to stop for a few moments throughout the day to notice and appreciate what's right in front of you. There's nothing you can do to change the past or foretell the future, so try to just enjoy the present with a mindful attitude. With continued practice, you'll find that being in the "now" has the potential to improve your anxiety-related symptoms.

6

Exposure Therapy

Now that you've explored CBT and mindfulness, let's examine another therapeutic approach to tackling social anxiety. In this chapter, you'll learn about exposure therapy and how it developed. Unlike CBT, which pays close attention to how our thoughts affect our behaviors, exposure therapy identifies what frightens us and encourages us to face those fears, often with the assistance of a therapist. Every person experiences anxiety over different things—maybe your anxiety is triggered when you attend a business meeting or when your boss asks you how a project is going. Or maybe your anxiety builds up when you have to meet a friend at a party. Every person is different, and exposure therapy encourages you to identify your personal fears and take steps to familiarize yourself with the fears to reduce their effect on you.

It's sometimes easy for those who don't have social anxiety to minimize your fears, pointing out to you that certain situations "shouldn't" be scary. You, in turn, tell yourself that you're ridiculous for being afraid of something. If you find yourself doing this, stop. Never invalidate your fears. Remember to be kind to yourself and practice compassion. Remember to feel pride whenever you face a fear, no matter how small it might seem to the outside world. And remember to celebrate the steps you take, regardless of the distance you cross. You can incorporate safe, step-by-step exposure therapy exercises into your daily routine in just a few minutes a day and take pride in your accomplishments. This chapter explains how.

QUICK QUIZ

Your sister just got engaged and asked you to be her maid of honor. At first, you feel excited and thrilled for her, but then you realize you'll be expected to make a speech at the wedding. Even though the wedding is still several months away, you find yourself worrying about the speech almost on a daily basis. What if you blush or start shaking while giving the speech? What if you stutter? What if your speech is boring or too short? You actually contemplate skipping an upcoming wedding that you've been invited to because it's such a daunting reminder of what's to come. Do you:

A. Choose to skip the wedding so you don't have to be reminded of what's expected of you at your sister's wedding?

B. Try to think of the positive aspects of your sister's wedding while ignoring the fact you have to give the speech, and attend your friend's wedding?

C. Choose to attend the wedding, knowing you won't enjoy yourself because you'll be worrying about your speech the whole time?

D. Start watching video clips of wedding speeches, writing drafts of your speech, and practicing them in front of close friends and family to help expose yourself to the experience? When you attend your friend's wedding, you take notes during the speech and visualize yourself giving your speech in that room.

Sometimes it's easier to ignore or avoid a situation or idea that provokes anxiety than to deal with it. However, that won't change the reality of a situation. If you selected A or B, your anxiety is causing you to avoid the situation. If you selected C, your anxiety is convincing you that you can't enjoy yourself. If you selected D, you might already be familiar with the concepts of exposure therapy. That's great. But don't worry if you're still feeling like you'd rather avoid the situation entirely. The information in this chapter will help you learn how to expose yourself to the anxiety-inducing situation to make it feel less daunting.

The Ins and Outs of Exposure Therapy

As mentioned, it's sometimes easier to avoid a situation than to confront it, even though that avoidance has its own negative feelings and consequences associated with it. Facing a challenging situation, though more difficult, is often the best course of action for overcoming avoidant behavior. That's where exposure therapy comes in. This therapy draws from behavioral studies developed by researchers like Ivan Pavlov, who pioneered the concept of classical conditioning in the early 1900s. (There is more on this topic to follow.)

Certain fears, anxieties, or phobias often thrive and develop further if that specific fear is continually avoided. Avoidant behaviors often occur in people with anxiety disorders, either in the form of avoiding the situation completely or choosing to only partially experience it. For example, someone with a fear of social gatherings may either avoid attending the gathering entirely *or* attend the activity but spend the entire time alone in a corner on his or her phone.

Exposure therapy encourages people to engage in fear-provoking scenarios and remain in the situation until the fear dissipates. Remember the earlier discussion of the flight-or-fight response? Fortunately, even if your body is flooded with this anxiety-inducing reaction to fear, it will eventually fade when you're able to identify that you aren't in any immediate danger. Remind yourself that even when you face your fear and feel that immediate wave of anxiety and distress, it will eventually fade and leave you with a stronger sense of strength and accomplishment. The more you're able to practice your own fear-facing capabilities, the more you'll find yourself facing your fears. This will provide you with a sense of control over your fears.

Exposure therapy can prove even more beneficial to a person who is also taking part in CBT. Someone who is resilient in identifying and understanding his or her thought patterns through CBT will be able to work on personal growth in conjunction with being exposed to the feared situation.

There are different forms of exposure therapy, which are listed on the following page. If you're interested in exposure therapy, you can work with a therapist to find the form of exposure therapy that has the potential to lead to the most progress. The therapist will likely design a program specifically to meet your needs. Nevertheless, you can still safely practice the exercises in this chapter on your own to get a feel for what exposure therapy is all about and even experience the benefits of this approach.

Understanding Classical Conditioning

In the early 1900s, the behaviorist Ivan Pavlov began studying the digestive system of dogs. During his study, he noticed that when the dogs heard sounds normally associated with mealtime, they'd begin to salivate. (Anyone who has a cat and pops the top off a can of cat food understands this familiar pet behavior!) Pavlov ran further tests on this response and stumbled upon what became termed "classical conditioning."

In his test, Pavlov rang a bell before feeding his dogs. He repeated this over and over until the dogs eventually began to salivate upon hearing the bell ring, whether or not food followed. A formerly neutral stimulus, the bell, became something that elicited a response in the dogs.

What this teaches us about behavior is that we can be trained through this reflexive form of learning. We can learn to associate certain stimuli with certain reactions. If you hear the term "job interview" and immediately feel dizzy, nauseous, or panicked, exposure therapy can help you learn to hear those words without experiencing anxious feelings. By exposing yourself to the elements of a job interview, you might eventually be able to hear the words and physiologically react in a calmer manner.

Different Kinds of Exposure Therapy

SYSTEMATIC DESENSITIZATION This form of exposure therapy pairs relaxation techniques with exposing an individual to fear-inducing thoughts or images, or the actual feared stimulus (the thing or event that provokes the reaction). It aims to change the subjective anxiety associated with the feared stimuli.

IN VIVO EXPOSURE Using a graduated design, *in vivo* exposure slowly exposes an individual to the feared stimulus in a safe setting. The therapist works with the client to develop the skills to interact with the feared stimulus in a healthy way.

VIRTUAL REALITY EXPOSURE This method incorporates computer programs and real-time digital graphics, which are viewed by an individual to place him or her in a simulated feared situation. The individual is connected to a biofeedback device to help gauge responses to feared stimuli, which allows the therapist to better align the exposure process.

Safety Behaviors

Safety behaviors are tactics people with social anxiety sometimes use to shield themselves in social situations in an effort to feel more secure. However, some safety behaviors might actually draw more attention to a person's unease. These behaviors become ingrained, and the likelihood is that someone with social anxiety might not even realize that he or she is engaging in a safety behavior.

The idea here is to become aware of your safety behaviors and how they affect the way you interact with the world. This is an important step in overcoming social anxiety. Sometimes you might think you're being open, but your body language says otherwise.

If You Only Have 5 Minutes
SPEAK TO A STRANGER

For the socially anxious, speaking to a stranger can be quite an overwhelming task. You might think you'll sound awkward and the stranger will think you're odd. Because you're already assuming a negative outcome, you might avoid asking for information you need, such as directions if you become lost. For this quick exposure exercise, set the intention to speak to a stranger. Perhaps you'll ask for advice on the best local lunch spot. Before you approach the stranger, take a few moments to check in with yourself. Keep in mind that, after the experience, you'll take time to think about how it went and how you felt about it. Try to be fully aware of your feelings and observations when taking the following steps:

1. Choose a public place where you feel comfortable such as a coffee shop, your favorite grocery store, or the local public library. A comfortable, familiar setting can make it easier to confront the scary situation.

2. Take a few deep breaths. Spend a few minutes practicing mindfulness. Pay close attention to the way your breath feels as it moves into your lungs. Take note of your feelings and thoughts with a nonjudgmental attitude.

3. As you scan the room for a stranger to speak to, pay close attention to any negative thoughts that enter your mind. Ask yourself if your thoughts are reality based. Replace any negative thoughts with more helpful thoughts, as discussed in Chapter 4.

4. When you have the opportunity, make a comment about your present situation, such as "The coffee here is great. Don't you agree?" Try to make eye contact while talking to the stranger.

When you've completed this activity, take a few moments to process the experience. How did you feel before you spoke to the stranger? How do you feel now? How long did it take for your anxiety to subside? Be proud of yourself for facing an anxiety-inducing situation and reward yourself for taking this first step.

Allowing your body to react in a way that defines a situation as scary may reinforce the fear and create even more anxiety. Even if you continually "expose" yourself to anxiety-inducing situations, if you repeatedly face the fear while also engaging in a safety behavior, it acts as a subconscious reminder that, yes, this situation is scary. Review the common safety behaviors below. Do any of them feel familiar to you?

Common Safety Behaviors

CROSSING YOUR ARMS The act of crossing your arms creates a physical shield between your vital organs and the outside world, which could come in handy in an authentically threatening situation. However, in a nonthreatening situation, it creates a barrier of sorts between you and others. Try to be conscious of when you cross your arms and ask yourself if you're doing it to "protect" yourself from a perceived fear. If you notice that your arms are crossed in a social situation, uncross them to show that you're available for interaction.

AVOIDING EYE CONTACT Making eye contact is an invitation to others to interact with you in some manner. For socially anxious people, the idea of social interaction is often anxiety inducing, so eye contact becomes minimal. By avoiding eye contact, you may be sending out a signal that you're uninviting or lacking self-confidence. If you find yourself avoiding other people's eyes, make an effort to meet their gaze from time to time as you interact.

STANDING AT A DISTANCE For those with social anxiety, it may sometimes feel safer to retreat to the outer edge of a room or to stand near a corner or in the back of a room. This behavior creates distance between you and others and draws attention away from you. Standing apart from the crowd makes it less likely you'll be able to hear conversations and perhaps join in or meet new people. If you find yourself engaging in this safety behavior, try to move closer to the center of the room.

TALKING FAST Socially anxious people sometimes speak quickly to get through a presentation or conversation faster to relieve their anxiety. This behavior may be the result of a negative core belief that what you have to say doesn't have worth. Be conscious of the rhythm of your speech, and if necessary, slow down. Remind yourself that what you have to say *is* important.

MUMBLING OR SPEAKING SOFTLY Some socially anxious people may mumble or speak too softly for others to hear without straining. This behavior may suggest to others that you aren't vested in the conversation. Mumbling or speaking without appropriate volume may be the result of feeling as if you have nothing to contribute or fearing that you'll say the wrong thing. If you suspect this is one of your safety behaviors, practice speaking clearly and confidently in a mirror. Then, when you feel comfortable, practice your speaking voice with a close friend or family member.

Public Speaking and Exposure Therapy

Public speaking presents a challenge for many people, but it can be especially challenging for people with social anxiety. Not only does public speaking require being the center of attention, but it also requires speaking with clarity and confidence. Since people with social anxiety generally struggle with these requirements, the prospect of public speaking can induce high levels of anxiety.

Common anxiety-related reactions to public speaking include nausea, dizziness, sweating, shaking, blushing, stuttering, and losing one's train of thought. For a person who is already concerned about being judged by others, public speaking can feel incredibly intimidating. This doesn't mean that a person with social anxiety can't become a good public speaker, of course.

If you're invited to make a presentation or give a speech, you can use this as a chance to practice exposure therapy techniques. To begin, it's especially important to be aware of any self-defeating thoughts or uncomfortable feelings you might have when thinking about the invitation. For example, in the earlier scenario in which you're faced with giving a maid-of-honor speech at your sister's wedding, a lot of energy was spent worrying about giving the speech. All of those anxiety-inducing thoughts can be unhealthy, as they're likely to cause your sympathetic nervous system to trigger the stress response. As you learned earlier, long-term exposure to stress hormones is associated with negative health consequences.

With an awareness of your self-defeating thoughts, list every possible negative outcome of giving the speech or presentation. Then objectively go through them one at a time. For example, say you're worried about stuttering. Ask yourself, *If I stutter during my speech, how would I feel? Would everyone laugh at me? Would they feel sorry for me? If they laugh, what would happen after that? If they feel sorry for me, what would happen after that?* Continue to ask yourself these questions, exploring every possible worst-case scenario for each of your worries. Keep in mind that even if one of the worst-case scenarios were to happen, you'll be stronger for having experienced it . . . *and* survived it.

With an idea of what you might be facing on speech day, begin to use your energy toward constructive tasks, such as practicing your speech in front of trusted friends or family. You can also practice your speech on your webcam or an audio recorder. Use this experience to redraft your speech if necessary so that it feels more natural or flows more smoothly. Continue to practice each revised version of your speech, both in front of other people and by yourself, until the words feel deeply familiar to you.

As you continue to practice, identify areas in which you show strength as a public speaker. For example, maybe your quiet voice will create a more intimate and relaxed feeling among the audience members or perhaps you have a good grasp of the topic and others can benefit from your knowledge. Look at the speech as a moment to share something with others; you're providing the audience with knowledge, a different perspective, a new lesson, or good wishes. View your audience as people who are rooting for you to succeed. Also know that many people are aware of how anxiety inducing public speaking can be, at least to some degree, so most people will likely empathize with you.

Visit the place where you'll be giving the speech or presentation, if possible. Visualize the room full of people and practice your speech out loud. See yourself succeeding, and feel the feelings associated with your success.

By breaking down public speaking into these smaller, more manageable practice steps, you're gradually exposing yourself to the experience. Each of the preceding steps will take you closer to your goal of giving a speech in public.

How Exposure Therapy and CBT Can Work Together

Exposure therapy and CBT are often used as overlapping treatments for social anxiety due to their similar goal of helping a person become more comfortable in social situations. As you may recall, CBT focuses on identifying the relationship between thought patterns and behaviors. When engaging in exposure therapy techniques, a conscious effort is being made to become more comfortable and calm around feared stimuli.

These two approaches complement each other by enabling a person with social anxiety to better understand how he or she thinks and feels about fear-provoking situations and then making a concerted effort to change his or her thoughts and behaviors to lead to a more fulfilling life. Consider the following example:

James, age 24, from Washington, DC, has struggled with social anxiety since grade school. He was teased a lot about his crooked teeth by his peers, which made him feel even more insecure. As a result of not wanting to bring any more attention to his teeth, which always resulted in bad feelings, he developed an intense fear of going to the dentist. He hasn't seen one since graduating high school. To make matters worse, now he's convinced the dentist will be angry with him for not coming sooner and will feel disgusted that James has never done anything about his crooked teeth.

James decides to consult with a therapist about his social anxiety and fear of the dentist. The therapist asks him to keep a journal to track his thoughts regarding his social situations as well as a potential dental appointment. Using the journal, James and his therapist analyze the source of James's negative thoughts and identify more positive thought patterns to replace the negative ones. In addition, the therapist has begun to show James photographs of dentist offices and dental instruments. After a few sessions, the therapist shows James actual dental instruments and asks James to hold them. As James interacts with the instruments, the therapist guides him in relaxation techniques. Soon, James is advised to visit a local dentist's office and set up an appointment to briefly interview the dentist in person. Setting up the appointment and then having the consultation are both low-stakes interactions, as neither task requires actual dental work.

Eventually, using the new thought patterns James has been practicing, along with the relaxation techniques he's developed when exposed to dental equipment, James schedules and attends a dental appointment.

Do you see how James and his therapist used both CBT and exposure therapy techniques to help James overcome his avoidance of the dentist? Are there any areas in your life where you might be able to use similar approaches? For example, identify a certain situation that you've been avoiding. What are your feelings surrounding this situation? What thoughts come to mind? What can you do to rephrase them to be more helpful? How can you expose yourself safely to this situation, one step at a time?

Assessing and Ranking Your Fears

If the graded approach to exposure therapy resonates with you, a good way to start practicing this technique is to rank your fears, which will guide you along the journey of slowly exposing yourself to higher-level anxiety-inducing situations. Think of the graded approach as a ladder. At the top of the ladder is the most anxiety-inducing situation you can possibly imagine. Each rung in descending order becomes less and less anxiety inducing, until you reach the ground level, which is your position before exposing yourself to any of the feared stimuli.

List your fears in your journal or on a piece of paper. They can be big or small. Think of every situation or encounter that has triggered your anxiety in the past. Next, using a rating system from 1–10 (1 being the least scary and 10 being the scariest), rate each item you've listed. By placing this list in descending order (everything rated 10 at the very top, counting down to anything rated 1), you'll have a visual representation of your "fear ladder."

Exposure Therapy Approaches
GRADED VERSUS FLOODING

There are two approaches to exposure therapy. Many therapists choose a graded approach, allowing an individual to rate his or her own comfort level with certain stimuli and work through being exposed to them slowly. Starting with stimuli a person fears only mildly, the client and therapist gradually work up to a higher-level feared stimulus.

Flooding, on the other hand, is much like the name sounds. A person is "flooded" with the higher-level feared stimulus at the very beginning of treatment. Instead of starting therapy by facing lower-intensity feared stimuli, it jumps straight to the one that causes the most distress in an effort to show the client, right away, that he or she can survive the situation.

To better relate to this, consider the following metaphor: You see two types of people at a pool or a lake; those who gradually step into the water, allowing themselves to adjust to the temperature, and those who jump in without first testing the water. The first person is taking the "graded exposure" approach, and the second is taking the "flooding" approach. Neither approach is necessarily better than the other, and both types of people are eventually exposed to the same water.

Evaluate your own personal comfort level with these exposure therapy approaches. Both are effective. If you choose to immerse yourself in exposure therapy, a therapist is an indispensable guide.

For example, let's say you listed *going on a first date* and rated it 10. That, to you, is when your social anxiety is triggered to its most extreme. Along with that situation, you've listed a variety of other situations that also trigger your anxiety, although not to the same degree. Your list might look something like this:

10. Going on a first date.

9. Asking someone out on a date.

8. Speaking with a person I find attractive.

7. Driving to the location where the date will be held.

6. Choosing an outfit to wear to the date.

5. Talking to a friend about the date beforehand.

4. Choosing where the date should be held.

3. Making eye contact with the person I find attractive.

2. Being in the same room as the person I find attractive.

1. Thinking about dating in general.

The list starts with the absolutely scariest situation and descends toward more and more manageable situations. That's not to say that an item ranked 1 doesn't still induce anxiety, but it means it's vastly more manageable than the anxiety induced by something ranked 10.

Once you've established a list of anxiety-inducing scenarios, you're ready to start slowly exposing yourself to them one at a time. In this case, you would start with the item on the bottom of the list: *thinking about dating in general.* Maybe this makes you a little nervous because it could eventually lead to a scarier situation. So, for starters, list the reasons the thought of dating elicits your anxiety. This will expose you to "thinking about dating in general" while creating a more objective and concrete activity around the idea, which will hopefully feel purposeful.

Once you feel your anxiety dissipate, you can graduate to the next rung on the ladder: *being in the same room as the person you find attractive*. While anxiety will inevitably be triggered by this situation, you can be aware of this and either practice CBT techniques beforehand or remind yourself that the anxiety will most likely fade after several minutes. Remember, the fight-or-flight response is trying to protect you from immediate danger. Eventually, your body will recognize that being in a room with someone you find attractive is not a life-threatening situation. You would then continue in this manner until you're able to reach the top rung.

Now that you understand how this process works in theory, spend some time creating your list and ranking your fears. Then, when you're ready, begin the process of slowly exposing yourself to the various situations you identified. Keep in mind that the more you repeat a certain "rung on the ladder," the more comfortable you'll become with that particular anxiety-inducing scenario.

Practicing Exposure Therapy Techniques

Exposure therapy works best when you're able to remain in a certain anxiety-inducing situation until you can feel your anxiety dissipating. Set goals for yourself in each situation. For example, if "meeting friends for dinner" provokes medium levels of anxiety for you, set up some parameters for the next time you choose to expose yourself to this situation. Maybe you need to stay for at least a round of appetizers, only check your phone once, or ask each friend how he or she has been. Hopefully, by the time you've accomplished each of these tasks, your anxiety will have faded, and you'll be able to experience the situation anxiety-free. Start small and work toward bigger goals, as explained in the previous section.

Before you jump into testing the waters of exposure therapy, be sure to keep a few things in mind: For starters, everyone makes progress at a different pace. Always celebrate the steps you're taking toward growth, regardless of how long it takes you. Second, it's okay to attempt to reach a personal goal several times before actually achieving it. Simply establishing goals is a strong step toward exposing yourself to feared stimuli.

Good Situations for Practicing Exposure Therapy Techniques

MINGLING AT A PARTY Parties are often attended by a mix of people; some you know, and some you don't know. Instead of going off into a corner, set a goal to speak with at least one new person. You can start by asking a simple question, such as "How do you know the host of the party?"

ATTENDING THE FIRST DAY OF SCHOOL Many teachers ask their students to introduce themselves on the first day of class. Just the idea of this can feel incredibly distressing to someone with social anxiety. Knowing that this is a likely question, practice your response in front of a mirror. If possible, visit the classroom a few days before classes begin to become more familiar with the setting. Imagine introducing yourself to the class, and visualize your classmates giving you a warm reception.

GIVING A PRESENTATION Reread the "Public Speaking and Exposure Therapy" section for some good, useable strategies for slowly exposing yourself to this anxiety-inducing situation. Practicing on your own and in front of a trusted friend can help ease some of your concerns.

If You Only Have 10 Minutes
HAVE A LUNCHTIME CONVERSATION

It's lunchtime at the office. All of your coworkers are congregating in the kitchen area. The light banter among your coworkers makes you feel anxious, so your usual behavior is to quickly retrieve your lunch from the refrigerator and hustle back to your desk. This is an excellent opportunity to practice exposing yourself to the situation. If you continue to avoid lingering in the kitchen, you're only reinforcing to yourself that the setting is scary. Remain in the kitchen for 10 minutes, making conversation with your fellow coworkers. Here's how:

1. Retrieve your lunch from the refrigerator and prepare it in the kitchen, rather than taking it back to your desk.

2. Make eye contact with your coworkers and comment on how delicious-looking someone's lunch is. Laugh politely at any jokes you hear.

3. Encourage yourself to ask a few questions to engage in the conversational banter while everyone is preparing their lunches or sitting down to eat. If you're feeling courageous, you might even ask to join them.

4. Before you leave, tell your coworkers you hope they enjoy their lunches or how nice it was to spend some time with them.

Afterward, take some time to evaluate how being part of the lunchtime experience, for even just 10 minutes, made you feel. How do you feel now that it's over? Did you notice your level of anxiety change at all during those 10 minutes? Spend a moment feeling proud of yourself for facing an anxiety-inducing situation you normally would have avoided.

TALKING TO AN AUTHORITY FIGURE Speaking with someone in a position of power can feel intimidating. If that person is a teacher or supervisor whose role involves evaluating your performance, it can feel even more so. To make an authority figure seem less intimidating, start by saying hello and smiling when you see him or her. You can then graduate to asking a question such as, "How is your day going?" Engaging this person in everyday "niceties" slowly exposes you to the idea of having a conversation with him or her.

GOING ON A JOB INTERVIEW During an interview, the interviewer is looking directly at you, evaluating you, and asking questions you might not be prepared to answer. With this in mind, it's understandable that even the idea of going on an interview can trigger anxiety. If you have a trusted friend or family member in business, ask if he or she will set up a mock interview for you at his or her office, so that you can safely expose yourself to the situation. Before this mock interview, find sample interview questions on the Internet and practice your answers.

USING A PUBLIC RESTROOM Many people do not like using a public restroom, but for someone with social anxiety, it can be especially distressing. If your social anxiety has led to an aversion of public restrooms and has resulted in discomfort, ease yourself into the experience by simply using the restroom to check your hair in the mirror or to wash your hands.

GOING ON A FIRST DATE Dating comes with a certain degree of vulnerability, which can feel very uncomfortable. The next time you have a date coming up, expose yourself to the idea of being vulnerable by calling the other person on the telephone prior to the date and sharing some lighthearted information about yourself. You might say, "Hi, I'm just calling to confirm the time and place for our date," or you might say, "I thought we could get to know each other a bit better before we meet."

TALKING IN A MEETING Whether it's in an academic or professional setting, speaking up during a group meeting requires a certain level of boldness. To expose yourself to how this might feel, practice interjecting during family dinner conversations or while hanging out with a group of friends. Using a person's name directly can help you ease into this. For example, you can say, "I agree, Bill. Here's what I would add to that . . ." And then share your ideas or opinions.

ASKING SOMEONE FOR A FAVOR When we ask someone to do us a favor, we are opening ourselves up for potential rejection as well as expressing our belief that we are worthy of receiving that favor—either of which could cause anxiety levels to rise. To avoid this, you might end up doing something alone when you could have used some help. To expose yourself to asking for a favor, start small by asking a friend or family member to help you make a meal that you can share together, or ask a coworker to proofread a letter you've written before sending it out.

HEARING CRITICISM It can be difficult to listen to someone point out your shortcomings and even more difficult if you spend a lot of time fearing the evaluation of others. To start exposing yourself to this fear, ask a trusted friend or family member to gently discuss areas in you where they see a potential for growth. Practice viewing this criticism in a positive light. Often, constructive criticism allows us to improve upon our shortcomings or strengthen our work.

SPEAKING ON THE PHONE There is an element of uncertainty that comes with speaking on the phone. You can't anticipate what the other person will say or how he or she will react or respond. Start with short, low-stakes phone conversations with close friends or family. You can also practice talking on the phone by ordering takeout food or making other purchases over the phone rather than ordering online.

Visualizing a Successful Encounter

You may want to consider mentally running through various scenarios until you arrive at a place in which you think you'll feel more comfortable in a real-life situation. This mental process is called visualization. It's used in a variety of situations, including professional sports. Athletes such as Olympic swimmer Michael Phelps have been known to spend time visualizing performing the motions of a particular event and imagining being successful.

You're equally capable of visualizing yourself in a challenging setting, one that tests your strength and perseverance, when taking your initial steps into exposing yourself to a feared stimulus. For example, let's return to the lunchtime scenario. To prepare to engage your coworkers in this situation, you can spend a few minutes at your desk visualizing the experience.

Your initial reaction might be to think of all the potential negative outcomes. Worst-case scenarios might come to mind, such as your coworkers laughing in your face when you try to engage them in conversation. Or you might imagine everyone awkwardly staring at you when you attempt to contribute to their conversation. Allow yourself to quickly exhaust all the negative potential outcomes, but then move on to the scenarios that end more positively. A coworker might give you the recipe when you comment on how delicious his or her meal looks. You might find something in common with a coworker with regard to a project you're both working on. You can visualize yourself laughing and authentically enjoying the conversation and interaction.

When you feel ready, you'll be able to transition from visualizing the scenario to experiencing the moment in real life or you might try *in vivo* exposure first by interacting in this fashion with your family at mealtime. Feel free to return to visualizing the situation as often as you feel is necessary to begin the initial steps of exposing yourself to feared stimuli in real life.

Saying "Yes" to Yourself When You Say "No" to Others

As you may know, a person with social anxiety often has a strong urge to avoid conflict. This might manifest as a perceived inability to say no in fear of a negative reaction or retaliation. Saying no is something you have to work up to by exposing yourself to the idea. One way to look at saying no to someone is to think of it as saying yes to yourself.

Imagine that you're having a really busy workweek, and you're looking forward to going to the gym and seeing a movie over the weekend. Then, a friend asks if you can watch her dog over the weekend. You know that your friend's dog requires a lot of supervision, and you really can't leave him alone for very long. That will spoil your plans to go to the gym and see a movie. If you agree to watch the dog, you're choosing to say no to yourself and your original plans to avoid conflict. By telling your friend that you'd really like to help out, but you have other plans, you're saying yes to yourself.

When you say no, pay attention to your reaction. Are you feeling guilty? Remind yourself that it's okay, and sometimes vital, to take care of your own needs before assisting with other people's needs. Yes, it's true that the person asking for the favor will probably be disappointed, and maybe even angry, if you say no, but the flip side is that you will be disappointed, and maybe even angry, if you say yes. So this is a matter of recognizing and respecting your own value. Saying no takes practice, but the sooner you start exposing

If You Have 30 Minutes

MINGLING AT A PARTY

If you're at a party where most of the other partygoers are unfamiliar to you, make an effort to briefly introduce yourself to various people. Of course being in a crowd of unfamiliar faces can feel scary, but remind yourself that any friends you have now were, at one point, strangers. With each interaction you have, you're exposing yourself more and more to engaging people you don't know in friendly conversation.

1. Before attending the party, list all the reasons you feel anxious about attending. You can even create a "fear ladder" as discussed earlier to get a good visual of what you find most uncomfortable about being at the party.

2. Establish several personal goals and/or parameters for the party that you'll encourage yourself to follow. For example, "I'll speak with two people before I grab a drink or a snack." Another goal might be, "I'll comment on how delicious the food looks at the buffet table." Make your goals realistic and visualize yourself achieving them.

3. While you're at the party, routinely give yourself a "pat on the back" for each goal you accomplish. You may even want to repeat a goal once accomplished for added exposure.

Take some time after the party to check in with yourself and think about how the experience felt. What was it like "exposing" yourself to a situation that usually causes your anxiety to rise? Did it feel surmountable? If not, what were your concerns? Remember to also focus on the positives of the experience. Simply making an intention to practice this exercise and taking the action necessary are good reasons to feel proud of yourself.

yourself to the experience of saying no, the sooner you can start saying yes to your own needs.

Now that you've learned how exposing yourself a little at a time can help you face anxiety-inducing situations head on, take some time to think about your typical day. Identify scenarios that typically trigger your social anxiety and pay attention to your thoughts and behaviors when you find yourself faced with those situations. Choose one or two common scenarios from your day when you can practice exposure therapy. Remember, take it one rung on the ladder at a time.

7

Meditation and Breathing Exercises

When it comes to finding relief from your social anxiety, meditation and breathing exercises can be enormously helpful. Much like mindfulness, meditation helps you learn to simply *be* without judgment. In this age of multitasking, much of our energy is focused on action, rather than on "simply being." In a person with social anxiety, and even for many people without social anxiety, a lot of energy is also spent on stressful thoughts about the past and future. Meditation and breathing exercises can help you quiet those thoughts and start connecting with your inner self.

Discovering who you are at your core is especially helpful for coping with any insecurities related to your social anxiety. This chapter echoes some ideas covered in the discussion on mindfulness, so use what you learned in that chapter to support and encourage this process.

QUICK QUIZ

A friend asks you to join her for a meditation class at the local community center. The instructor will lead the class in a guided meditation. Since your anxiety has felt a little unmanageable lately, you decide to give it a try. Within minutes, you realize your mind isn't quieting. In fact, your thoughts feel louder than ever. You feel self-conscious and wonder if anyone notices that you're having difficulty. You wonder what's wrong with you because everyone else in the room seems peaceful and calm. Your anxiety starts to build, and you feel yourself blushing in embarrassment. Do you:

A. Allow your thoughts to spiral out of control and eventually decide to leave the class halfway through?

B. Allow your thoughts to spiral out of control, but remain seated through the remainder of the class, despite feeling like a failure?

C. Allow your thoughts to spiral out of control for a few minutes before making an effort to listen to the instructor? You may not know what to do, but you can always listen.

D. Allow yourself to observe your negative thoughts, but then bring your awareness back to the present moment? You make an effort to keep trying even if you keep having setbacks.

It's common for newcomers to meditation to feel frustrated by the process and to have unrealistic expectations of clearing their minds of all thoughts. This may lead them to believe that they are "incompatible" with meditation. If you selected A, B, or C, you might have doubts about your ability to successfully meditate. If your thought patterns habitually lean toward the negative or unhelpful, it's only natural you'll resort to this "comfort level" of thinking when attempting a mindful activity such as meditation. If you selected D, there's a good chance you aren't new to meditation. Regardless of how you responded, you'll find helpful and inspiring tips on how to practice meditation in a manner that can help relieve your anxiety.

Meditation 101: The Basics

If you are new to meditation and hope to make this mind-calming practice part of your daily routine, start by choosing a special place to practice in every day that offers limited distractions and allows you to focus on yourself. It doesn't need to be a large area; a corner of your living room, a bench in your garden, or an area in your bedroom would all work. The point is to establish that this is your meditation sanctuary. See it as a welcoming space in which to practice.

You can choose to sit or stand. You want to be comfortable, but the space should also be functional. For example, the cushioned armchair in your living room may be comfortable, but maybe you have a habit of falling asleep in it. Or maybe a wooden chair helps you sit upright, but your back starts to hurt after a few minutes. Neither of these would be the best choice. Try out a few different options to determine what works best for you. You might feel intimidated by the idea of starting a meditation practice, but keep in mind that all you need is your mind, body, and a quiet place to sit or stand.

Types of Meditation

There are various approaches to meditation, including guided meditations, transcendental meditation (commonly called TM), Buddhist meditation, Native American power animal meditation, Taoist meditation, focused meditation, mantra meditation, and so on. From this brief list, you can see that there are many types from which to choose! Some meditations are intended to channel your focus toward loving-kindness, feeling grounded, clearing negative energy, and/or connecting with your inner self and the world around you. For starters, begin with the 10-minute self-compassion meditation or the 30-minute meditation described later in this chapter. Then, as you become more comfortable with the idea of meditating, you can start exploring other types. When you find one that resonates with you, you'll be well on your way to developing a regular practice.

Determine a length of time for your meditation. If you're just starting out, five minutes may be all you feel ready to do. You may eventually want to work up to a half hour, but even five minutes will be beneficial. Set a gentle alarm for yourself so that you don't keep looking at the clock.

When you're ready to begin, go to your space, and structure your body in a state of purposeful calm in the following manner: Imagine that your head is being gently lifted toward the sky. Engage your back and core muscles so that they support your body. Check in with your physical being by performing a quick body scan. Relax the muscles in your face, jaw, shoulders, arms, and legs. Bring your awareness to your breath, focusing on how the air feels as it moves into your nostrils, down into your lungs, and then back out into the world. How does your breath sound? What is the temperature of the air as it flows in and out of your body? Can you feel your stomach expanding and your chest rising with each inhalation and contracting with each exhalation?

Be compassionate with yourself as you continue to acknowledge the action of your breath in this manner. Your mind may start working overtime, but don't let that discourage you. Observe your thoughts and allow them to pass by like clouds in the sky without trying to grab on to them or judging them. A common misconception is that you shouldn't think at all during meditation, but it's virtually impossible to stop the thoughts from coming for very long. There are other misconceptions as well. Take a look:

Common Misconceptions about Meditation

MEDITATION IS THE SAME AS HYPNOSIS While meditation and hypnosis may seem to share qualities on the outside, they are dramatically different in one big way. The purpose behind hypnosis is to induce a trance-like state. Hypnosis is intended to bring you into a place of heightened focus and concentration, sometimes for the purpose of remembering one incident very clearly or for therapy-related assistance, such as quitting smoking. Meanwhile, meditation is intended to bring your awareness fully to where you are in the moment with a focus on your inner self.

MEDITATION IS A METHOD OF RELAXATION The process of meditating is relaxing, but there is more to it. To experience the benefits of this practice, it's important to be in a relaxed state *before* beginning. Therefore, as you prepare to meditate, take a few minutes to calm yourself by breathing deeply and intentionally releasing any tension in your muscles.

MEDITATION IS ZONING OUT Some assume that meditation is about becoming oblivious to everything that's going on around you and inside your mind. As mentioned earlier, clearing your mind completely—zoning out—is unlikely. The goal of meditation is to learn to control your thoughts and emotions so that you can experience a state of peace. You'll still be aware of noises and sensations, but you'll simply allow them to drift away.

MEDITATION IS A RELIGIOUS PRACTICE Meditation takes many forms. Although the practice has its roots in Buddhism, many approaches to meditation have evolved over the years and embrace every kind of lifestyle.

MEDITATION ISN'T FOR PEOPLE WITH ANXIOUS, OVERACTIVE MINDS
When living in a state of frequent anxiety, it can feel daunting to imagine quieting your mind and connecting with your inner self in the moment. Maybe you've given meditation a try at one point and felt it was impossible to control your thoughts. However, meditation is just like any other form of "exercise." You'll need to build and strengthen certain muscles over time to become more and more skilled at the exercise. Would you expect yourself to be able to run a marathon without any training? Be patient with yourself, and take it one moment at a time.

Breathing Exercises

Breathing exercises can be a quick way to center yourself before you enter an anxiety-inducing situation or just to calm down when you're feeling anxious. They're also helpful when preparing to meditate. Breathing is a symbol of consistency that we carry with us everywhere. Our breath grounds us and is a shared experience with everyone around us. If you find your anxiety building up and start feeling as if you're lacking control over your thoughts and emotions, remind yourself that your breath is a steady, supportive presence. Use your breath in times of stress as a reminder that you're never alone. Your breath is always with you, and you have the power to slow it down, listen to it, and use it for comfort.

One of the easiest ways to bring awareness to the breath is to identify the type of breath you're taking. For example, does your breath feel "shallow" or "deep"? A shallow breath is a breath that only reaches your chest and the oxygen only reaches the top of your lungs, which results in less oxygen being transported to the rest of your body. You want to support your body with adequate oxygen, which means you want to practice breathing more deeply.

Place a hand on your heart and a hand on your stomach. Take a few breaths and see which hand moves more. If you are breathing deeply and filling your abdomen with oxygen, the hand on your stomach will rise and fall the greatest amount.

The breath connects every part of the body. It regulates heart rate, blood pressure, oxygen levels, and digestion. It assists the body in communicating with the brain and vice versa. This is why breathing exercises are such a great step toward managing social anxiety. When your sympathetic nervous system is triggered by your anxiety, your body might develop a "mind of its own." By taking control of your breath, you're signaling your body to listen and relax.

⑤ If You Only Have 5 Minutes
LISTEN TO YOUR BREATH

One of the most important first steps in beginning a meditation practice is to bring focus and awareness to your breath. If your anxiety is building, tuning in to your breathing may help you quickly relieve your symptoms. Follow these steps:

1. Ground yourself in a stable position by sitting in a chair or standing with your feet hip-width apart.

2. With your mouth closed, breathe in deeply through your nose, paying close attention to how the breath feels. Listen to it moving into your body. Then, breathe out through your nose, again paying close attention to how it feels and sounds.

3. On your next breath, breathe in for three slow counts, hold your breath for three slow counts, and release for three slow counts. Pay attention to the way your body moves as you breathe in and out.

4. On your next breath, imagine that you're breathing in positive energy, light, or pleasant images. As you exhale, imagine that you're pushing out negative thoughts or emotions from your body. Repeat the visualization until the five minutes are up.

Upon concluding this exercise, check in with yourself. What did you notice about your physiological reaction? How does your heart rate feel? Throughout the day, it helps to remember that your breath and body are connected. Take a moment now to contemplate how efficiently your blood transports the oxygen you inhale throughout your entire body. Remember, this oxygen fuels you for every situation you encounter.

Using Affirmations During Meditation

Affirmations are statements that, when repeatedly regularly, help reinforce positive beliefs. For example, if you struggle with a lack of confidence in social situations, spend a few moments repeating to yourself, *I'm strong and confident when interacting with other people*. Affirmations help create new thought patterns and beliefs that can positively influence your behavior and comfort level in social situations.

You might find the following affirmations useful for channeling your focus toward positive thoughts during meditation. You can use one or a combination to personalize your practice.

- I'm worthy of happiness.

- I'm unique and beautiful.

- I deserve respect.

- I listen to my heart.

- I deserve to have my voice heard.

- I'm capable of sharing love.

- I believe in myself.

- I'm intelligent.

- I trust my feelings.

- I'm a strong, independent individual.

- I deserve peace of mind.

- I'm enough.

Take a few moments to come up with a few affirmations that resonate with you at the present moment. Maybe you're going through a particularly challenging time at work right now or your patience

If You Only Have 10 Minutes
SILENCING YOUR INNER CRITIC

Your inner critic is the part of you that's always pointing out that what you just did is totally wrong or, at the very least, not quite right. The one that sometimes shouts, sometimes whines, sometimes whispers—but always with the same basic message: *You're just not quite up to par. You're flawed, and it's embarrassing. What's wrong with you?!* When you notice that your inner critic starts taking center stage in your mind, take a quick 10-minute break to practice this self-compassion meditation.

1. Find a quiet place where you can comfortably sit without distraction, such as the meditation space you identified earlier.
2. Take a deep breath, and settle in. Rest one hand over your heart and the other on your belly. Say "ahh" to release the tension in your jaw. Breathe.
3. Allow the voice of the inner critic to arise. Allow the emotions that it triggers to arise. Can you experience the emotions as simply bursts of life-force energy? Can you hear the inner critic's words as simply sound—a kind of music, like a Mozart string quartet, just not quite as harmonious? If so, great. If not, no problem. Simply notice and allow the thoughts and emotions to be, like the sky allowing clouds space to float.

4. Now offer words of kindness and compassion to yourself. The inner critic is just one member of the committee. Now it's time to give the floor to your inner advocate: the one who offers words of support. You write the script, and you step into that role. Even better, let it be your "wisdom mind" that's speaking. You know how to do it. Say, "I love you unconditionally." Say, "You are primordially pure." Say, "No human being is perfect, and I love and accept you just the way you are."

When your 10 minutes are up, notice how you feel. Do you feel more compassionate toward yourself? Can you remember to remind yourself from time to time how much you truly do love and accept yourself? If you can make this a habit, you'll feel yourself softening around the edges and may find that some of your social anxiety is easing up.

is being tested at home by one of your family members. Whatever the case may be, craft a few affirmations that speak to your heart to help you deal with that particular situation. Also identify other situations in which your anxiety usually manifests and create specific affirmations for those occasions as well.

Once you have a few well-crafted affirmations that feel good to you, practice repeating them out loud or in your head throughout the day. You might consider looking at yourself in a mirror and saying them to yourself. You can also use them when you're meditating. For example, if your mind wanders to negative thoughts, bring your attention back to the meditation by repeating one of your affirmations. Hopefully, in time, you'll begin to believe what you're saying. Just keep at it.

Don't Try to Force the Benefits

Sometimes when you enter into a new activity, such as a meditation practice or breathing exercises, with the wrong mind-set and/or not enough information, you can do more harm than good. Consider the scenario in which you chose to attend a meditation class with your friend. Although your initial goal was to reduce your anxiety through meditation, it actually ended up increasing it in this scenario. Your thoughts ran amok, and you immediately assumed there was something wrong with you. This fed a negative core belief such as "I'm not good enough," which resulted in more anxiety and discomfort. The negative core belief was reinforced. If you selected the first choice in that scenario, your anxiety escalated to the point where you chose to leave the class in an unhappy state. This might have turned you off from meditation entirely. Had you felt an urgency to "get it right," you likely would have been equally disappointed.

If You Have 30 Minutes
MOVE PAST ROADBLOCKS

When living with social anxiety, you might spend a lot of time thinking about a painful memory from your past, because the socially anxious mind has a habit of replaying such scenarios over and over again. This 30-minute meditation practice will help you move past this incident, enjoy the present, and focus on a positive future.

1. Find a quiet place where you can comfortably sit without distraction, such as the meditation space you identified earlier.

2. Close your eyes and bring awareness to your breath. Pay attention to how your breathing affects your heart rate.

3. Scan your body in a manner that allows you to connect with every area of your physical being. Relax your muscles, particularly those in your face, neck, and shoulders, to bring your body to a comfortable resting place.

4. Imagine that you're standing on a pathway in a heavily wooded area. The trees are tall and thick and line the pathway in front of you. Spend a few moments breathing in the crisp, forest air and listening to any sounds you hear.

5. When you're ready, visualize yourself walking down this path, taking note of everything around you. As thoughts or worries enter your mind, simply observe them and bring your awareness back to the wooded path.

6. Now, imagine that you come across several large stones in your pathway. Each stone represents a painful memory from your past. Take a moment to closely observe each stone, identifying the memory and focusing on how everything is concentrated within this hard, solid stone.

7. Select one of the stones and pick it up. Feel the weight of this memory in your palms.

8. When you're ready, turn and place the stone off the pathway, nestled within plants and other rocks. Stand back and appreciate that the stone looks more at home in its new resting place than it did on your path.

9. Repeat steps 7 and 8 as many times as you need to until all the stones in your path have been cleared away.

10. Continue walking along the path, observing that up ahead is a brightly lit clearing. If you encounter any other stones, or memories, along the path as you move forward, repeat steps 7 and 8.

11. As you approach the clearing, start to feel the warmth of the bright light. Step into that warmth and breathe in the sunlight as it embraces you.

12. Spend a moment appreciating the sunlight, imagining that it represents all your strength and potential. Remain in this clearing for as long as you like and feel free to explore the area. When you feel ready, bring your awareness back to your breath.

13. Listen to the sound of your breath entering and exiting your body, while wiggling your toes and fingers. Take a moment to thank yourself for taking the time to practice meditation. When you're ready, open your eyes.

You may find yourself feeling energized after completing a longer meditation session or you may feel a little drained. Either way, take a few minutes to check in with yourself to notice how you feel, physically, emotionally, and mentally following this meditation. Make observations, but try to avoid judging your experience.

Meditation and breathing exercises are not about meeting a specific goal or experience. Instead, they're giving you an opportunity to simply be present in the moment. So be aware of your state of mind when you're trying these activities. If you hear yourself starting to think "should" statements or feeling as if you're doing something wrong, just pause and bring your awareness back to your breath. Remind yourself that you're giving yourself the gift of developing a new skill, and it will take time to overcome some of your knee-jerk reactions.

Where Meditation Can Take You

So much of living with social anxiety is defined by the repeated, harmful thought patterns that disrupt the ability to lead a fulfilling life. Your mental and physical health may be negatively affected by an inability to release your negative thoughts. Whether it's a weakened immune system, general fatigue, a sensitive stomach, or something else, anxiety finds ways to affect your health. Meditation is a good way to start clearing your mind of negative patterns so that you can begin to enjoy better health.

Meditation has no harmful side effects. A regular practice has the ability to help decrease depressive thoughts, relieve anxiety, and increase positive thoughts. For example, in a study performed by the University of South Carolina and reported in the journal *Integrative Cancer Therapies*, researchers found that anxiety levels were reduced in women undergoing radiotherapy for breast cancer who took part in an eight-week MBSR program. At John Hopkins University, more than 18,000 studies on meditation were reviewed with over 35,000 participants; reviewers found evidence of improved anxiety in those who practice meditation, as reported in the journal *JAMA Internal Medicine*.

Let's revisit the concept that meditation is a form of exercise that's helping you build up certain muscles. Specifically, meditation strengthens your ability to regulate your emotions and thoughts. How? Here's a hypothesis: During meditation, the part of the brain that manages thinking and emotion, the anterior cingulate cortex, is activated. This assists meditators in tracking, assessing, and regulating their self-referential thoughts (thoughts one has about oneself). It connects the thinking muscles to the emotional muscles, giving meditators more power to determine which direction their thoughts take, especially in the way they think about themselves.

When it comes to meditating, all you need is yourself and a quiet space. You can choose when, where, and how you meditate. Just simply give yourself the opportunity to engage in the meditation exercises suggested in this chapter without having any expectations and without judging your experience afterward. Practice your meditation muscle for just five minutes at a time, and soon you'll likely experience the benefits of a calmer mind. Simply breathing during your meditation practice is the only requirement. Remember, your breath is your lifeline.

Practicing Gratitude

Gratitude has been receiving a lot of attention lately. In fact, showing gratitude almost seems like the fashionable thing to do these days and for good reason: Being grateful for both tangible and intangible things provides a variety of health benefits—from strengthening your immune system to increasing your level of compassion for others and yourself.

In people with social anxiety, negative thought patterns commonly interfere with experiencing feelings of gratitude. Take a quick look back at the negative thought patterns discussed in Chapter 4. A common theme among them is that you're at fault in some way. This cycle of negativity may lead you to believe that there isn't much to be grateful for. However, this can change. Consciously choosing to be grateful, or practicing gratitude, helps disrupt the cycle of negativity by shifting your focus away from what might be wrong to what's right in your life.

QUICK QUIZ

A friend invites you to a pick-up basketball game at your neighborhood park. Even though you haven't played in a while and are feeling a little insecure, you decide to head over and see how it goes. Good for you! But then halfway through the game, you're crippled with embarrassment over how poorly you're playing. Your teammates haven't said anything, but you're convinced they're blaming you for the reason your team is losing. You keep missing passes, and when your friend asks if you're okay, you say, "I'm out of practice. I should just go home." Your friend points out what a beautiful day it is and reminds you that you're all there to have fun. Do you:

A. Roll your eyes at your friend's failed attempt to be positive and go home?

B. Appreciate your friend's attempt to be positive, but go home anyway?

C. Appreciate your friend's positive attitude and stick around for the game, while still beating yourself up for your poor performance?

D. Appreciate your friend's positive attitude and continue playing, grateful for the opportunity to have fun on a beautiful day?

Negative thoughts can interrupt an otherwise positive experience. In this scenario, can you take a moment to step back and appreciate the positives of the situation? The day is beautiful, you have leisure time, your legs and arms work even if you can't catch a pass, and so on. If you selected A, you're probably having difficulty seeing past your anxiety. If you selected B or C, you may be grateful for your friend's attempt to make you feel better, but you aren't actually practicing gratitude—in other words, you aren't seeing that there truly is much to be grateful for in this situation. If you selected D, you likely already know some of the skills of practicing gratitude. That's great, keep it up. If not, keep reading. You'll learn how to develop an attitude of gratitude!

Why Practice Gratitude?

Practicing gratitude is a way to recognize the abundance in your life when you once might have only noticed emptiness. Let's say you have just moved into a new apartment, but you haven't furnished it yet. On your first day, you stand in the living room. You could look around and point out everything that's missing. *There isn't a single piece of furniture in here*, you might think. The room is empty, and you begin to think about everything you don't have and need to buy. On the other hand, you could look around and acknowledge everything you have. *I'm so lucky to have a roof over my head*, you think instead. You know that not everyone has an opportunity to live in an apartment, and standing in the middle of it fills you with gratitude for all the possibilities.

In the two versions of this scenario, the apartment didn't change. It's just an empty space. However, the way you choose to look at it will either make you feel as if something is lacking or make you feel fortunate. For people coping with social anxiety, life can often feel like it's missing something. Your anxiety may cause you to focus on everything you don't have. You may find yourself having thoughts such as: *I should have more friends* or *I wish I could find a better job*.

Research has shown that practicing gratitude increases overall well-being. The University of Pennsylvania Positive Psychology Center, as cited by the Harvard Health Article "In Praise of Gratitude," performed a study in which 411 people composed letters of gratitude and delivered them to recipients. The letter writers reported a dramatic increase in happiness levels. On the other side of the country, the GGSC at the University of California, Berkeley teamed up with the University of California, Davis to launch a three-year project called "Expanding the Science and Practice of Gratitude." Since its launch, the project has developed the online journal "Thnx4.org," which allows users to keep their own gratitude journals while also tracking and sharing their gratitude. In 2012, $3 million was awarded in grant money to studies that hope to better understand gratitude, such as how it can affect romantic relationships and friendships. In addition, in 2013, it awarded 15 grants for research on gratitude, including its effects in the workplace and on health.

Researchers at the Greater Good Science Center found that people who keep a gratitude journal every night experience a more optimistic outlook on life and deal better with adversity. They also found that gratitude can strengthen romantic relationships. When people spend time communicating why they are grateful for their partners, they feel an increase in positive emotions toward their partners and feel better about their relationships as a whole.

In addition, studies have shown a wide variety of health benefits in people who regularly practice gratitude in their daily lives. Start practicing gratitude to reap the following benefits:

The Health Benefits of Practicing Gratitude

- Strengthened immune system
- Lower blood pressure
- Increased optimism
- Increased compassion
- Increased generosity
- Decreased loneliness

By making a conscious effort to practice gratitude, you are not only improving your mental health, but also your physical health. In this way, gratitude can complement a healthy diet and exercise routine (see Chapter 12 for more on diet and exercise). As with all the strategies discussed in this part, practicing gratitude can be used in tandem with other strategies to help you see positive results in your daily life.

Being Grateful for Your Anxiety

You probably view your anxiety as something to fight or something to rid yourself of. Anxiety can interrupt your life in tiring and discouraging ways. It has a habit of repeating itself in a manner that can make you feel as if you have no say in the matter. The moment you feel you've conquered your anxiety in one form, it can crop up in another area. For example, let's say you've been working hard to expose yourself to the social interaction of making eye contact with strangers. You have made great progress and feel proud of yourself for being able to make eye contact at least a few times throughout your day. But then you notice your anxiety is starting to build up over whether or not you'll have to shake hands

If You Only Have 5 Minutes
TAKE STOCK OF YOUR GRATITUDE

In the morning, before you start your day, take stock of everything you have to be grateful for. This doesn't have to be an exhaustive list, just a quick rundown. Then, if you encounter an anxiety-inducing situation during the day, you can bring to mind the abundance in your life to settle your anxious feelings. Here's how:

1. Upon waking in the morning, spend five minutes listing things in your life for which you are grateful. You can write this list in a gratitude journal or on a piece of paper. Otherwise, just taking note of the list in your head is enough to create the good feelings associated with expressing gratitude.

2. Start small, such as being thankful for a bed to sleep in, for your pillow and blankets, for the sun outside your window, and so on. Then move on to more specific and larger things such as job to go to and a healthy family.

3. With your feelings of gratitude in mind, remind yourself that no matter what the day ahead has in store for you, you'll always have something to be grateful for.

Beginning your morning with gratitude can help you set a positive tone for the day. Throughout the day, notice how you feel. Does the day seem a little brighter to you? Are you able to recall what you are grateful for when you feel your anxiety levels rising? If you find that you can't, a written list can be helpful for next time.

with someone at your upcoming meeting. What if your hands are sweaty? What if you go to shake someone's hand and the other person leaves you hanging?

It's easy to wish your anxiety would "just go away." However, an anxiety disorder, while manageable, is something you'll likely be living with for the rest of your life. This can feel even more defeating. Fortunately, it doesn't have to be. Consider this example:

Jameson, age 34, from Houston, Texas, has struggled with social anxiety since adolescence. He spent the majority of his high school years volunteering in classrooms during his lunch break to avoid socializing with his peers. He can recall feeling furious with himself for being so anxious and wishing his anxiety would go away. Things didn't improve once he was in college; if anything, they got worse. He would rush from his dorm room to classes and then back to his dorm room, avoiding speaking with anyone around him. He spent a lot of his nights studying, even when he didn't have to, and dwelled on how much his anxiety was controlling his life. He'd feel upset that his anxiety seemed to be keeping him from living a more fulfilling life.

Upon graduating college, Jameson got a job at his family's property-management company. He continued to struggle with social anxiety, so he focused on rising through the ranks rather than on connecting with his coworkers. Over the years, Jameson has become more and more resentful of his anxiety and uses a lot of his energy being envious of people who seem to have an easier time interacting with others.

If Jameson could learn to not only understand, but also *appreciate* his anxiety, he might be able to turn his perspective on life around. It's difficult to change an opinion after feeling negative toward something for so many years, but that doesn't mean Jameson wouldn't be able to do it. Instead of looking back on his life and wishing things had been different, he could identify the ways in which his anxiety has possibly helped him over the years. While, yes, it was an obstacle to being more outgoing or making more social connections, it did allow him to reach other achievements. It gave him a chance to be a helpful volunteer to his teachers throughout high school. It was the reason he studied so hard in college and why he was able to enjoy the benefits of the promotions at his job. If he practiced gratitude, Jameson could try to find ways to be thankful for his anxiety rather than resenting it. He could see his social anxiety in a more welcoming light.

When you try to fight something, it can become a larger, scarier presence. The very *idea* of your anxiety may cause more anxiety. Negative emotions can spawn more negative emotions. So try to embrace your anxiety in a positive light and feel gratitude for what it has contributed to your life. Maybe it has made you a more empathetic person or taught you to be a better listener. Maybe you can reach out and help those around you who are also anxious. Your experience is unique to you and has taught you special lessons about yourself and others. This is no small accomplishment.

Affirmations of Gratitude

Much like mindfulness, gratitude reminds us to be present in the moment and notice what we have versus what we lack. Practicing gratitude can help you replace negative thoughts with positive ones, and in this way, it draws on the CBT techniques you learned about in Chapter 4. If you need reminders of how to be in a mindful place of gratitude, practice repeating one or more of the following affirmations at various times throughout the day:

- I'm thankful to be given another day on this earth.

- I'm thankful for my breath.

(10) If You Only Have 10 Minutes
WELCOME YOUR ANXIETY

If you feel your anxiety beginning to interfere with your day, your knee-jerk reaction may be to feel frustrated by your reaction or with yourself for not being able to deal with your feelings. You probably just want your anxiety to go away. Instead, take a few minutes to welcome your anxiety as if it's an old friend. Here's how:

1. Acknowledge that your anxiety is present and say hello to it as if it's an old acquaintance making another appearance.

2. Suggest that you'd rather not spend time with it today, but if it insists on sticking around, you'll be happy to have it there.

3. Thank your anxiety for reminding you that you're capable of experiencing strong feelings. It's a powerful physiological and emotional reaction, which means you're capable of great feats.

4. Feel grateful that your anxiety has helped you appreciate what you're capable of.

While this practice may feel foolish at first, even counterintuitive, you might discover that it helps alleviate some of the fear or dread you associate with the onset of your anxiety. As mentioned, sometimes the fear of becoming anxious can actually trigger anxiety. If you view your anxiety as something to be thankful for, you might not fear it as much. Give this quick exercise a try to see how you feel afterward.

- I'm thankful for being able to educate myself about anxiety.
- I'm thankful for what my anxiety has taught me about myself and humankind.
- I'm thankful to be able to try to overcome social anxiety.
- I'm thankful for myself.

Affirmations of gratitude can be practiced anywhere at any time. If you find yourself worrying as you drive to work, try replacing your thoughts with affirmations of gratitude for having a working car. If you're about to go on a date and are convinced your date won't like you, replace this with an affirmation of gratitude for the opportunity to practice your dating skills. The possibilities are virtually limitless.

Sharing Your Gratitude with Others

When was the last time you thanked someone? Social anxiety has a tendency trap you inside your head, locking your focus on your own troubles and negative thinking. One of the best ways to quickly connect with the outside world or with another person is to simply thank someone. Saying thank you is like extending a warm hug without physical contact. It's a way of communicating appreciation, acknowledgment, and connection.

Social anxiety can foster feelings of loneliness. You may end up withdrawing or no longer reaching out to people with whom you were once close. This type of social withdrawal can lead to depression. (See Chapter 10 for more on this.) To help counteract this, make an effort to show the people in your life that you truly appreciate them. Whether you tell them verbally, write them a thank you letter, or send them a small gift, be sure to express *why* you're thankful. You can start tomorrow morning by thanking the person

If You Have 30 Minutes
SEE THE BIG PICTURE

Sometimes it takes looking at the big picture to start appreciating the smaller things in life. Draw on what you have learned about meditation practice, and take the following steps:

1. Find a quiet, comfortable place such as the meditation space you identified earlier.

2. Close your eyes, bring awareness to your breath, and quickly scan your body and relax any tense muscles.

3. Contemplate yourself as a singular being for a few minutes, and then expand your contemplation to include your family, friends, coworkers, and acquaintances.

4. Slowly continue to expand your focus, slowly and consciously, so that it encompasses the vastness of your neighborhood . . . then your city . . . then your state . . . then your country . . . then your continent . . . and finally the whole world.

5. Now imagine that you're observing the whole of humanity from space. Use this opportunity to appreciate how incredibly interconnected we all are.

6. Continue seeing this "big picture" image with gratitude in your heart, and then zoom back in to yourself, feeling grateful for being an important part of this larger whole.

7. When you're ready, wiggle your toes and fingers, and then slowly open your eyes.

When your anxiety is causing you to have repetitious negative thoughts, you can lose focus on the bigger picture. Use this exercise as a reminder that your very existence and your part in the larger whole is something to be grateful for.

who makes you coffee by saying, "Thanks! This is a great way to start the day," or the stranger who holds the door open for you by saying, "Thanks! That's so thoughtful of you."

Through the act of saying thank you and expressing why you're thankful, you'll likely start to feel your gratitude blossoming. It will strengthen your social connections and help you engage in a positive manner with the people in your life. If you want to find a way to increase your feeling of interconnectedness, start by showing gratitude to someone you appreciate.

Another manner of sharing your gratitude and developing a feeling of interconnectedness is "giving back." You can donate time or resources to a worthy cause. This helps pull you outside yourself and connect with the world around you in a positive manner. Is a charity in your neighborhood looking for volunteers? While your social anxiety may make you adverse to the idea of volunteering, remind yourself that this selfless expression of gratitude will increase your happiness and decrease your anxiety.

When sharing your gratitude with others, try switching your perspective so that you view everything you do as a gift given and/or received. This may sound odd since a gift is often thought of as a tangible item that comes wrapped in colorful ribbons. However, the act of spending quality time with someone can be a gift you give to each other.

Start shaping your actions and behaviors into a form of gift giving and receiving. When you smile at someone and someone smiles at you in return, you're exchanging the gift of an open, positive response. When you have a conversation with someone, you're giving each other the gift of a listening ear. Viewing your interactions as gifts can help you become more mindful in your everyday actions and see yourself and others in a more altruistic light. In the end, this will likely encourage you to be even more grateful, giving, and open to possibilities.

Building Confidence and Assertiveness Skills

As you learned in Chapter 2, SAD is different from shyness. Shyness is a reaction to a new or uncomfortable social encounter. Social anxiety, on the other hand, is a prevalent type of anxiety that doesn't only arise in the presence of someone new, but before, during, and after the encounter (in many different types of social situations), thereby disrupting the quality of life and everyday routines. While it may not always be obvious, most people who have social anxiety genuinely like people and want to establish meaningful relationships. If you're reading this book to learn how to cope with your social anxiety, you probably agree with that assessment. You also know that social anxiety can often make it a struggle to be confident and assertive around others.

People with social anxiety can be energetic, spontaneous, engaging, and emotionally invested in those around them. However, it can be a challenge for some with social anxiety to find a happy common ground between their desire to be social and the negative thought patterns that hold them back from living a more active social life. The lack of confidence one might feel can be a frequent source of frustration.

If you're lacking in confidence and assertiveness and feel ready to learn how to strengthen these important social skills, spend some time exploring this chapter and giving the exercises a try.

QUICK QUIZ

You're at an outdoor concert with several close friends. Crowds mill around on the lawn, and you find yourself laughing effortlessly at your friends' jokes. You're feeling confident and happy. But then you suddenly notice a person a few feet away from you that you think is very attractive, and you'd like to get to know him or her. For a split second, you imagine yourself going over to say hello, but then your anxiety gets triggered. You blush and your breathing becomes labored. You quickly feel any and all confidence you had a second ago evaporate from your body. Do you:

A. Move further away from the attractive person, withdraw emotionally from your friends, and spend the rest of the concert beating yourself up for not being more confident and outgoing?

B. Tell yourself the person you find attractive wouldn't be interested in someone like you and identify one of your friends who would be better suited for that person, then spend the rest of the concert silently resenting that particular friend's carefree nature?

C. Spend a few more minutes observing the attractive person as you begin to imagine worst-case scenarios as well as scenarios that might not end so badly?

D. Acknowledge your anxiety, take a few calming breaths, and inch nearer to the attractive person with the intention of catching his or her eye so that you can attempt to say hello?

If you selected A, B, or C, your anxiety has a way of ruining a moment that had been full of exciting possibilities. It also has a way of ruining the rest of the evening. If you selected D, your anxiety is still present, but you're also exercising your "courage muscle" as you take a few steps closer. If you feel like this muscle could use a little more power behind it, keep reading.

What Is Confidence?

It may be easy to look at someone who is opinionated, loud, and aggressive as possessing the quality of confidence. Oftentimes, this is how confidence looks to people with social anxiety. You might find yourself envying those who seem comfortable speaking up in large crowds or contributing to conversations. However, according to authors Katty Kay and Claire Shipman of *The Confidence Code*, it turns out that confidence isn't based on attitude; it's based on taking action. For example, someone who routinely voices his or her opinion loudly in crowds may actually be overcompensating for feeling insecure about those opinions. Volume of voice doesn't necessarily illustrate confidence, although it may seem that way to a socially anxious person.

Confidence comes from acknowledging that, although something seems scary to you or causes you to feel uncertain, you can still take action toward your ambitions and desires. The more you take action, the more you'll learn that you can survive anxiety-inducing or unfamiliar situations. Over time, you will build more and more confidence. Being able to identify, feel, and believe in your own power spurs you to move forward with confidence. This takes time, but for now, try the following quick tricks to help you feel more confident on the spot:

Tricks to Feel More Confident

ACKNOWLEDGE YOUR LIMITS Go into an anxiety-inducing situation understanding and accepting that you don't know everything, which is perfectly acceptable. You can never completely prepare for an event or encounter. Keep in mind that no one else in this situation knows everything, and no one is entirely prepared for the surprises of life or the course of events. This sooner you understand this, the sooner you can take action.

STAND LIKE A SUPERHERO Place your feet hip-width apart. Allow your arms to hang at your sides or rest them on your hips. Lower your shoulders, raise your chin, and place a slight smile on your lips. Simply standing in a confident manner will influence how you feel. (There's more on body language later in the chapter.)

LOOK AND DRESS THE PART Before heading out to a social function, take a shower, primp a little, and put on a nice outfit. Looking your best can immediately boost your confidence level. Choose clothing in which you feel comfortable yet powerful. When you look at your reflection, see yourself as you are: capable of taking action.

RECALL A TIME WHEN YOU FELT CONFIDENT Upon entering an anxiety-inducing situation, or before going in, bring to mind a situation in which you felt confident. Feel in your body and mind how that felt and hold on to that feeling as you interact with others.

How Perfectionism Affects Social Anxiety

A large part of social anxiety is rooted in the fear of being closely watched or judged by others. This may lead people with social anxiety to focus on trying to be perfect in an effort to avoid criticism. They likely don't realize the paralyzing effect perfectionism can have on them and their behaviors.

There is a difference between the desire to excel and the desire to be perfect, according to Paul Hewitt, a professor of psychology at York University in Toronto. Hewitt has spent a great deal of time researching the idea of perfectionism and some of the problems that arise from the desire to be perfect, which include depression, anxiety, and even suicide.

Some argue that there are two types of perfectionism: adaptive and maladaptive. In other words, the first type can have positive effects and the other negative effects on growth. However, others believe that perfectionism shouldn't be looked at as adaptive at all because perfectionism comes with a sense of fear that, if one isn't perfect, he or she will be rejected by others. Either way, striving to be perfect creates feelings of helplessness and hopelessness, because there is simply no way to be perfect.

If you're struggling with a need to be perfect, it's important to begin practicing acceptance of who you are—flaws and all. It's vital to nurture your feelings of self-acceptance even in light of what you might perceive as imperfections. Telling yourself or another perfectionist to "stop trying to be so perfect" only increases feelings of inadequacy. If your desire to be perfect interferes with living your life, consult with a health-care professional who is trained to assist you.

Understanding the "Spotlight Effect"

Many of our behaviors and thoughts are based on survival. This is how human beings have been able to thrive and grow over the millennia. Our individual actions are intended to ensure that we, as individuals, have the greatest chance of survival. However, this creates an often-overlooked phenomenon: each of us is the center of our own universe.

This isn't to say that we're all selfish—far from it. We can still live compassionate, empathetic lives that allow us to support and help humankind, while looking through the lens of our own experiences. While most people wouldn't point at you and say, "You are the center of my universe," it can sometimes feel like everyone around you is focused entirely on what you do and say. This is called the "spotlight effect." Here is an example:

Jocelyn, age 17, from Omaha, Nebraska, was rushing to class on her first day of college. She'd spent extra time that morning selecting a "perfect" outfit and left her house early to make sure she wasn't late to class. Despite leaving early, she ended up missing the bus and had to wait for the next one. As she began worrying about being late to class and making a spectacle of herself, she could feel her anxiety building. Once she finally found her classroom and slipped in the back door, she spent the rest of the class convinced that everyone was thinking about the fact that she was late and calling her a slacker in their heads. Even the way the professor looked in her direction convinced her that he was disappointed in her.

In this scenario, Jocelyn is experiencing the spotlight effect. She is overestimating the degree to which others notice her actions and behaviors. She feels as if a spotlight is shining on her and her actions. Have you experienced this phenomenon? Think back on your past week. How many times did you find yourself genuinely noticing and/or critiquing the behaviors of others? If you did notice the behaviors of others, how much time did you actually spend contemplating them?

More often than not, people are generally more focused on themselves and their own experiences than on what other people do and say. People with social anxiety might beat themselves up for doing something they wouldn't even notice if someone else were to do it. When you find yourself feeling self-conscious or embarrassed in a certain social situation, remind yourself of the spotlight effect. Try to view the situation objectively and ask yourself how you would feel if you were watching yourself from a distance. More likely than not, there is no "spotlight" in sight.

Familiarize Yourself with Body Language

Our bodies often communicate to others more than we realize. Understanding body language can help you develop better social skills. Try this exercise: the next time you have a one-on-one encounter with a close friend, pay particular attention to how he moves. As your friend approaches, analyze how he is holding his body. What does it seem to say? Since this person is a friend, most likely he will be approaching you in an open and friendly manner. But maybe not. Maybe he had a defeating day. Are his arms at his side or casually tucked into his pockets? How does his face look? Is he smiling? If not, what does his expression say to you?

Simply take note of all these things. As you converse or go about your activity, see if any of your observations change. If this is a close friend, go ahead and ask him what he noticed about your body language. This may spark a frank conversation about body language and how best to communicate to others that you're open and friendly.

If you want to take a more calculated approach, sit in a public place (a mall, airport, or park works great) with a notebook in hand. Observe people as they go about their day. What do you notice about body language in general? Are there any patterns? Can you identify when someone seems to be in a hurry? In a bad mood? Excited to be going somewhere? Jot down some of your observations. Following this exercise, begin to casually pay attention to body language as you interact with the people in your daily life.

On your path to managing social anxiety while also building your confidence, be aware of your own body language. This isn't about becoming critical of your movements, but rather about increasing an awareness of when you're closing down and when you're opening up. This is similar to the same way CBT encourages you to be aware of unhelpful thoughts so that you can replace them with helpful thoughts. When you become aware that you're indicating to others through your body language that you aren't interested in engaging them socially, a simple shift of your body can turn that around.

Confident Small Talk for
a Greater Return

It's common for someone with social anxiety to dread the "small talk" that's often experienced at social functions. For someone with social anxiety, it can feel taxing and mundane to think of questions to ask complete strangers and, in turn, answer the questions that are asked of you. While other people may brush it aside and not even notice small talk, people with social anxiety can walk away from a conversation feeling bad about themselves. They may feel resentful that the conversation felt pointless and therefore was a waste of their time.

Small talk can leave a person feeling this way because it's just that: small. There is usually very little depth in small talk, and it can make a person feel like the people involved in the conversation don't actually care about the answers. For someone who feels drained by conversation, regardless of the topic, small talk can be a cause of negative feelings.

It's okay to feel this way about small talk. Don't spend time beating yourself up for disliking trivial banter. Instead, craft questions you can ask of others that will elicit more in-depth answers or connections. Show a person that you're truly listening and respond by asking something that can potentially take the conversation a little deeper.

Small talk is a social convention that's usually used as a form of greeting. Remind yourself that it's a stepping-stone that generally must be crossed before you can engage in more in-depth conversations. Remember to show empathy for the person on the other side of the conversation. Instead of shrinking away from the small talk,

(5) If You Only Have 5 Minutes
MIMIC A CONFIDENT STANCE

In the same way that engaging in the safety behaviors discussed in Chapter 6 can undermine your ability to overcome your social anxiety in a particular situation, your body language can sometimes directly influence your level of confidence. A confident stance can breed confidence, even when you aren't feeling quite so brave. The next time you're feeling less than confident, take a few minutes to adjust your body language by following these steps:

1. Pause for a moment to notice how your body is currently positioned. How are you holding your shoulders? Are they stooped? Are you slouching? Are your arms crossed? Are you gazing downward? It's helpful to do this in front of a mirror if one is available.

2. Now, ask yourself how confident people hold themselves. Imagine how they stand, where they place their arms, and how their heads and necks are positioned. What is the expression on their faces?

3. Try to mimic a confident stance, whatever that looks like to you. As you make adjustments, keep in mind that you want to communicate that you believe in yourself and your abilities through your body language.

The more you practice moving your body in ways that reflect confidence, the more natural this will feel to you. You can enlist the aid of a trusted friend to help you figure out what positions, both sitting and standing, look most natural and exude the most confidence.

look at it as an offering of connection. By engaging in the small talk, you may be doing the other person a favor. For all you know, that person walked into the situation afraid that nobody would want to talk to him or her.

If you feel uncomfortable with small talk and/or find yourself craving more in-depth conversations, brainstorm some questions that garner more complex answers. If your goal is to get to know someone better, don't be afraid to dig a little deeper. Consider the following:

Sample Questions to Get Past the Small Talk

- "What was the best part about your day today?" (Follow-up question: "What made it so great?")

- "You mentioned that you're an architect. How did you become interested in architecture?" (Follow-up question: "Have you ever thought about doing something else?")

- "You mentioned that you're going hiking this weekend. Do you normally spend your free time in nature?" (Follow-up question: "If you could hike anywhere in the world, where would it be?")

At first, this may feel a little forced since you may not be used to engaging in "bigger" small talk, but if you're someone who dreads small talk, asking questions that go a little deeper is worth a try. The person on the other end of the conversation will probably appreciate the refreshing questions. The more you practice asking questions and following up with additional questions, the more natural this will begin to feel. And the more natural it feels, the more confident you'll feel taking this action toward making social connections.

If You Only Have 10 Minutes
TRACK PATTERNS OF INACTION

Have you noticed any patterns of inaction due to a lack of confidence? If you think about it, there's a good chance you'll see that there is a pattern to your inactivity. One of the best ways to analyze these moments is to document them in your journal. Follow these steps:

1. At the end of the day, list any moments you recall wishing you had the courage to take action on behalf of your desires or goals.

2. Take note of who was present, how you felt, and why you think you didn't take the desired action.

3. Describe how you want to act in a similar situation in the future. Be specific and truthful. For example, maybe you won't necessarily be ready to take the lead at a meeting, but you'll be able to communicate your opinions or ideas in a clear voice to your coworkers.

4. Return to this journaling activity whenever a new situation arises in which you didn't take a desired action or when you want to compare your progress to an earlier situation.

By recording the situations that tend to dampen your confidence, you can start to better understand the circumstances that trigger those moments and become aware of the patterns. With this awareness, you'll be able to prepare better for those particular situations.

Understanding Assertiveness

Assertiveness shares commonalities with confidence in that it often requires action. When you have social anxiety, it can be difficult to assert yourself by sharing your thoughts, opinions, and needs because you don't want to draw attention to yourself or cause conflict. You may find yourself routinely being the accommodating one. Do you find yourself going along with the crowd most of the time? If someone asks you where you'd like to go for dinner, do you find yourself answering, "Wherever you want to go"?

While it may seem easier in the moment not to assert yourself, in the long run, being passive invites others to take advantage of you. It also reinforces any negative core beliefs you may hold about yourself of not feeling worthy. You may feel unworthy of being heard, of sharing your opinions, or of influencing someone's decision.

Think of the people in your life you care about. Now, imagine that they tell you they don't think their opinions matter. What would you tell them? Of course, you'd want the people you love to be able to speak their minds and feel safe and validated while doing so. Now, imagine one of these people is you. What would you tell yourself? Remember that you possess the ability to stand up for your rights, while still respecting the rights of others. You are worthy and valuable, and your opinion matters.

Australia's Centre for Clinical Interventions (CCI) offers a helpful resource for improving assertiveness skills on their website. In one of its teaching modules, CCI identifies the following four assertiveness techniques:

Types of Assertiveness Techniques

BASIC ASSERTION By identifying your needs and clearly expressing them, you're engaging in basic assertion. Try to eliminate qualifying statements or unnecessary additions to your statement and be as clear as possible. For example: "I need to leave tonight at 6:30."

EMPATHETIC ASSERTION This type of assertion not only acknowledges your own needs but also acknowledges another person's perspective. This is a good approach when trying to find a compromise. For example: "I understand you don't feel like stopping your activity, but I need you to help me with dinner. Then you can go back to your activity."

DISCREPANCY ASSERTION When an agreement has been met in the past, yet the current situation doesn't reflect this agreement, you may need to employ discrepancy assertion. This is a way to clarify a situation that may feel contradictory to you. For example: "It was my understanding that this assignment needed to be completed by Friday; however, now you're asking for it on Wednesday. Please clarify the correct deadline."

NEGATIVE FEELINGS ASSERTION It's best to use this form of assertion when your feelings toward another person are negative, as it enables you to both acknowledge the situation and voice your feelings. For example: "When you interrupt me while I'm talking, I feel like my voice doesn't matter. In the future, I'd appreciate a chance to complete my thought before you respond."

As you become more familiar with the different types of assertiveness techniques, think about the situations in your everyday life when you might have a chance to practice these important communication skills. Rather than bottling up your opinions and needs, which may only increase your anxiety, tap into your inner source of confidence and let your voice be heard. You can never know how another person will react, but that's okay. When you're being assertive and exercising your freedom to say what's on your mind, you're giving other people the opportunity to say what's on their minds as well. Remaining silent shuts down the lines of communication and potential resolution.

Assertive "I" Statements in the Form of Self-Disclosure

Sometimes you can be assertive simply by stating how you feel. This basic form of assertion is commonly referred to as the self-disclosure technique. This means you reveal something about yourself that others may not know. The purposes of these statements are to reduce anxiety. By saying something out loud, you're no longer using energy in an effort to hide it. You're eliminating the potential fear, anxiety, and embarrassment that might be associated with the statement. It's a way to take back control over something that seems to be trying to control you.

This might come in the form of the statement, "I feel anxious." Say you're about to present a project in front of a classroom of your fellow students. As you walk up, you can feel your cheeks start to burn and your hands begin to shake. You know everyone will notice, and you wish you could hide it. However, since you know you can't hide your nervousness, you instead start your presentation by playfully stating, "Wow, I feel nervous being up here in front of you." Your classmates chuckle a bit, and since your anxiety is now out in the open, you can get on with your presentation—even if your voice shakes. You're no longer wasting mental space worrying if any of your classmates will notice that you're blushing. Instead, you can focus on the hard work you put into the project.

10 If You Have 30 Minutes
PRACTICE "I" STATEMENTS

When you practice being assertive, it's important to become familiar with helpful ways to phrase your thoughts and emotions. When you feel the need to be assertive in a certain situation, it's likely that you're also experiencing deep emotions about something. Practicing being assertive will help in real-time situations. Engage the help of a trusted family member or friend to be your partner for this exercise, and follow these steps:

1. Brainstorm a few scenarios in which you'd like to be more assertive.

2. Spend time crafting helpful "I" statements and try them out on your partner. For example, the scenario may be something like you feel ignored when you return home from a long day at work by someone in your family. Maybe you think the statement, "I feel like you never listen to me" is assertive and helpful, but your partner might advise you that he or she would be more receptive to the statement, "I feel frustrated when you don't pay attention to me when I get home."

3. Practice various "I" statements for each scenario you identified to determine how the statements make you feel. Do you feel assertive? What feedback are you receiving from your partner?

It may feel unnatural at first to clearly and concisely tell someone how you feel or how his or her actions make you feel. Listen to your body's reactions when you practice being assertive. Try to understand what negative emotions are at the core of this particular case of anxiety. This exercise can lead to an honest conversation with your friend or family member in which you invite that person to share his or her perspective on your struggles with assertiveness.

Being assertive and taking action with confidence may stir up anxiety for you. You might fear that others will be upset with you for expressing your opinion or following through on what's important to you. People who respect you, whether or not they share your views, will applaud you for valuing your own self-worth. Practice speaking your mind around people you trust. If someone asks where you want to go for dinner, pick a restaurant! Being confident in your actions and assertive around people who care about you will help you take the next step toward being assertive and confident around coworkers, strangers, and those in authority. All of this requires action. You *can* do it.

CHAPTER

Quality Alone Time versus Isolation

As you've been learning throughout this book, social anxiety can cause you to create avoidant behaviors. When you associate social situations with anxiety, discomfort, or distress, you might tend to avoid social events all together. However, avoidance only reinforces the behavior. It looks like this: You choose to stay home rather than attend a social event because you feel comfortable and safe at home. You use your comfort as reinforcement that the social event would have been just the opposite: uncomfortable and scary.

The problem with this kind of behavior is it starts to build upon itself over time. The more you avoid social events, the more you'll feel distant from them and the more uncomfortable you'll become with the idea of joining them. You might start to feel lonely or isolated, and due to your lack of socializing, you might not have many people to reach out to. This cycle is familiar to many people living with social anxiety, and it can feel difficult to break free from. It can also lead to depressive feelings. Look at it this way: the quieter you become, the harder it is for people to hear you. The less you reach out, the less people will take your hand to help. While all relationships are symbiotic and require efforts and energy from both sides, do your best to recognize if you're routinely withdrawing from the outside world. In this chapter, you'll learn what often contributes to isolation and how you can energize yourself to engage in more social activities, while keeping in mind that alone time also has its benefits.

QUICK QUIZ

Your cousin sent you an invitation to her husband's birthday party. Although you feel touched that she remembered to invite you, you wish she hadn't. It feels like more energy than it's worth. You won't know anybody there, and you'll have to drive an hour out of town to get to the restaurant where the party is being held. You know the parking lot of that particular restaurant is really tight, and you think to yourself that you probably won't even be able to get a parking spot. You also realize that it's a Friday night—the end of the workweek. You'll be tired anyway, you tell yourself. Do you:

A. Decline the invitation, convincing yourself you would prefer to stay in that night and watch a few of your favorite TV shows alone?

B. Decline the invitation and spend the night feeling guilty for not going to the party because it might have ended up being fun?

C. Decline the invitation but ask a few of your closest friends if they'd like to come over to watch a movie with you that evening?

D. Accept the invitation, telling yourself you might meet some interesting people at the party, and it will be a good opportunity to practice engaging socially with others.

It can often feel safer to stick to your usual routine than to venture out into a social situation. Sometimes you might just genuinely prefer to be alone; other times, you might be letting your social anxiety make the decision for you. It's important to pay attention to your habits. Try to determine whether or not your habits are encouraging growth or keeping you stagnant. If you selected A or B, chances are you're allowing your social anxiety to keep you isolated. If you selected C, perhaps you really would rather be with a small group of people than attend a party. If you selected D, you've been taking the steps throughout this book. Bravo! In any case, it's important to know the reasons for declining an invitation. You truly might need some quality time alone—or you may be isolating yourself due to your social anxiety.

The Difference between Quality Alone Time and Isolation

Solitude comes with many benefits. In a world where we are often bombarded with visual stimuli, noises, demands, and obligations, it can become almost vital to carve out quality alone time for yourself. But, for some reason, the need to "get away" has developed an almost negative association. You hear words like "break down" and "recovery" thrown around in even the most casual of instances when someone chooses to step away from a challenging professional role or life event. However, spending time with yourself is important for your mental and emotional health.

When you step away and spend time alone, you allow yourself space to process what's going on in your life. You can think deeply about how you feel and shape more informed decisions for yourself. Maybe you aren't sure how to react to the way a certain person treated you. By allowing yourself the space to process the situation, you may come away with clarity and self-assurance. Solitude can give your mind a much-needed break and improve your ability to concentrate and be more efficient upon returning to the "real world." Solitude is purposeful and mindful.

On the other hand, isolation is the withdrawal from others without a healthy purpose. It's based on fears, insecurities, and anxiety. This type of isolation doesn't benefit your quality of life and can prove to be harmful. If you aren't benefiting from being alone, then it's not "quality alone time." Review the following list and be honest with yourself:

Signs You May Be Suffering from Isolation

AVOIDING SOCIAL SITUATIONS FOR AN EXTENDED PERIOD OF TIME If your alone time has persisted for an extended period, and you're feeling lonely as a result, you may be suffering from isolation.

LOW FEELINGS OF SELF-WORTH Do you feel like you aren't worthy of having friends or intimate relationships? Try to identify negative core beliefs that may be causing you to isolate yourself. (See Chapter 4 for more on negative core beliefs.)

POOR EATING HABITS Often when a person stops taking care of his or her emotional needs, he or she also stops taking care of his or her physical needs. Have your eating habits changed for the worse?

Poor eating habits are a symptom of isolation. Try to determine if your change in diet has anything to do with how you've been feeling socially.

LOSING CONTACT WITH CLOSE FRIENDS If you find yourself no longer reaching out to your closest friends and family members, you may be struggling with isolation. When was the last time you spoke to your closet friend or family member? Make an effort to reach out to someone you trust and let that person know how you've been feeling.

Keep in mind that feelings of isolation can be experienced even when you're surrounded by people. If you don't reveal at least part of yourself to others, you can still feel isolated and alone despite being in their company. Keeping yourself closed off or on guard is a defense mechanism. Opening up to others requires you to be vulnerable, which increases the potential for being hurt. It's understandable that you want to protect yourself; however, sometimes the consequences of doing so far outweigh the benefits. (There's more on this later in the chapter.)

What to Do When Quality Alone Time Is a Choice

Throughout this book, you've been learning about how to interact with people more comfortably in social settings. The simple fact that you're reading this book means that, even if you have been isolating yourself, you're ready to take steps to bring yourself out into the world. But this doesn't mean that sometimes you won't need quality alone time. Just keep in mind that the keyword here is "quality." Take a look at a few great ways to interact with yourself that can add quality to the time you *choose* to spend on your own.

Good Activities for Quality Alone Time

HIKING Hiking not only benefits you with physical exercise, but it allows you to reconnect with nature and expose yourself to new, exciting scenery. Challenging yourself with a particularly long hike offers a sense of accomplishment at the end of the trail.

JOURNALING Journaling is an excellent way to spend some quality time with yourself. The process of transferring your thoughts into written words is an exercise in self-awareness and will help you better understand yourself. In fact, many of the exercises in this book recommend journaling as a self-awareness tool.

JOGGING OR BIKING Explore your neighborhood or city while also getting some beneficial cardiovascular exercise. Jogging or biking is a great way to spend some time reframing your thoughts and possibly working through some recent challenges.

TAKING A NEW ROUTE If you take the same route to work or school every morning, change things up a bit. Find a route that will expose you to new scenery and pockets of your neighborhood you might not have known existed.

Do you gravitate toward a certain activity when you're feeling in need of some alone time? Take some time to think about this activ-ity. What about it appeals to you? How do you usually feel after you have completed this activity? If you start to feel bored with your usual activity, try something new and see how that affects your mood.

If You Only Have 5 Minutes
CONNECT THROUGH MUSIC

Let's say you've been feeling particularly disconnected from other people, and you feel anxious and out of touch. Now is a good time to take five minutes to establish a connection with the outside world through music. Here's how:

1. Choose your favorite relaxing or upbeat song. Put in ear buds or find a private place to enjoy the music.

2. Play the song and allow your thoughts to focus on the music and lyrics. Listen with all your attention.

3. Take this time to reconnect with humanity. Do you have any special memories connected to the song? Does someone you know also enjoy this particular song? What feelings does it elicit in you?

4. When the song is over, spend a moment thinking about your answers to the questions in step 3. Music has a beautiful way of bringing people together.

Listening to music can help ease your anxiety by redirecting your mind toward something you enjoy. It also connects you with other people's feelings. Taking five minutes to listen to an uplifting song is something you can do virtually anytime.

Feeling Lonely While Surrounded By People

As mentioned earlier, feelings of loneliness and isolation can be experienced even when you're surrounded by people. For example, imagine that you're standing among a crowd of people, and everyone is discussing a movie that just came out in theaters. You also saw this movie, and you feel like there might be a chance to join the quick-paced conversation. However, your voice feels frozen in your throat. You're about to say something, but then someone else interjects. You chide yourself for not getting the timing right. What you had to say is no longer on topic, so you listen closely and search your mind for something else to say. But no one is looking directly at you anyway. They aren't even asking for your opinion, it seems. You feel invisible. You start to wonder if what you have to say would even be important to them. In the end, you just smile and nod, waiting for the uncomfortable situation to end. Not only do you feel out of place but you also lonely, despite being surrounded by people.

For the socially anxious, feeling alone despite being in a crowd can be a frequent, uncomfortable experience. Even having background knowledge on the topic of conversation doesn't seem to help in many cases. Social anxiety can make you feel trapped and unable to share or contribute to any conversations. This can then result in the feeling that you're not being heard or even that others don't notice you.

Keeping quiet is a way of trying protecting yourself from the judgment of others. As you've learned, people with social anxiety frequently stress over what people think about them. (See "Understanding the Spotlight Effect" in Chapter 9.) The more someone knows about you, it seems the more there is for them to

10 If You Only Have 10 Minutes
BRAINSTORM ACTIVITIES

If you've become stagnant and/or comfortable in your usual routine, it may feel daunting to try to think of something outside the norm to do. Take a few moments to jot down ideas so you can refer to the list the next time you're seeking an activity. Be sure to include activities you can do on your own as well as with other people. As you make an effort to be more comfortable socially, try to strike a balance between alone time and time spent with others.

1. In your journal or on a piece of paper, brainstorm various activities you can take part in, whether as quality alone time or with other people.

2. Think about what you might do if a friend from out of town visited. Research free activities offered in your area. A picnic in the park is always a nice idea. Are there any classes or activities you might want to try? What interests you? A cooking class or pottery class might be fun. Or maybe you'd be interested in volunteering. Think about what type of volunteer work interests you—dog walking at your local shelter or helping with a fund drive, perhaps.

3. Keep this list easily accessible so that you can use it as a guide if you start feeling lonely or if you feel like trying something new.

Sometimes just the act of thinking of ways to become more engaged with your community will spark action. And by documenting your ideas, you can eliminate the potential roadblock of sitting and thinking, *I don't know what to do today.* With this list, you'll have plenty of choices!

judge. This leads to feelings of vulnerability and the fear of getting hurt. It's understandable that you want to protect yourself from getting hurt by remaining quiet and/or keeping yourself isolated, but in the long run, the consequences of isolating yourself can far outweigh the benefits.

How Loneliness Can Lead to Depression

Many people living with anxiety disorders report feeling symptoms of depression. This is because the two disorders share a lot in common. For example, those struggling with depression often become focused on their own problems and become locked into a cycle of negative thinking. This is very similar to the thinking patterns of people living with social anxiety. People living with depression also tend to withdraw from social events, which is a common trait in those struggling with social anxiety.

People who feel a strong sense of community are less likely to experience symptoms of anxiety or depression. While you may be able to acknowledge the importance of fostering close relationships and engaging in social communities, it may not be as easy to execute if you're dealing with social anxiety. Let's say a friend keeps inviting you to the movies on Saturday evenings, but you never feel up to going. Soon, the friend stops inviting you, and you identify that as reinforcement that he or she never liked you in the first place. When the invitations stop, you start beating yourself up for not accepting. You may feel upset with yourself for not "being better" or for not "trying harder." In the end, this can turn into a negative cycle of feeling bad about yourself, which can affect your other relationships.

If You Have 30 Minutes

WRITE A LETTER

People with social anxiety often find that they're better able to express themselves in writing. If you're feeling trapped in loneliness or are trying to figure out how to help someone understand you better, take some time to write a thoughtful letter. Here's how:

1. Think of a person in your life with whom you would like to share parts of yourself. Use stationery or work on your computer.

2. Compose a letter that's open and honest, and communicates at least some of what you've been going through, but also what you want to share about other parts of your life. Craft the letter with the goal of feeling better known by the recipient.

3. Mail or hand deliver the letter to the recipient and let him or her know you look forward to a response.

It can be frightening to open up part of ourselves to another person. However, the more we open up to the world around us, the more it will open for us. By showing courage and allowing yourself to feel vulnerable, you might inspire other people to reciprocate the behavior. This can help you feel more connected and supported by the people in your life.

If you're feeling lonely due to social anxiety, that loneliness may accumulate over time and result in feelings of depression. Be conscious of how your social anxiety affects your sense of loneliness and seek help immediately if you suspect that you're suffering from depression.

It's healthy for people to seek out solitude from time to time. It's important to create safe, purposeful moments for yourself when you can process your day, understand how you feel, and simply enjoy your own company. However, it's also important to be conscious of how beneficial and persistent your alone time is. If you start developing feelings of loneliness or isolation, take steps to connect with the people in your life and your community. If you feel severely depressed, seek help from a health-care professional.

11

Natural Remedies

Anxiety-relieving natural remedies, such as relaxing scents, oils, teas, and supplements, can make a good addition to your SAD treatment plan. This chapter provides an overview of some available remedies on the market so that you know what to look for and how they might help. The good thing about natural remedies is that many of them are simple, convenient, and easy to use throughout the day. This way, even if you're at work or a social event, you can still turn to your natural remedy for on-the-spot support.

The Natural Way

Always keep in mind that no person's experience with social anxiety is exactly the same as another's. Each of us is unique, so one person's response to a remedy will invariably be different from someone else's. Therefore, it's important to consult with a health-care professional before starting any new treatment, natural or not. Just because something says "natural" doesn't mean there are no risks involved. Some natural remedies might interact with medications or should be avoided if pregnant or breast feeding. Also, be aware of the possibility of allergic reactions while exploring natural remedies. Again, explore these options under the guidance of a health-care professional.

With that in mind, if you're looking for a new, natural approach to managing your social anxiety or are hoping to supplement your current one, spend some time reviewing the list below to see if any sound appealing. Over time, you may discover a personal approach to using natural remedies that works best for you to help combat your social anxiety. Test out a few different methods and pay attention to how they make you feel.

Natural Remedies for Combating Social Anxiety

DECAFFEINATED HERBAL TEAS Caffeine can increase anxiety, so when you're seeking out a cup of hot tea, reach for a calming variety of herbal tea. Chamomile and mint tea are well known for their soothing effects on the nerves.

ESSENTIAL OILS Derived from certain herbs and other plants, pure essential oils are a good way to experiment with the healing effects of aroma. Certain oils are known for their stress-relieving, calming properties. When using an essential oil topically, be sure to

The Importance of Sleep

According to the ADAA, not getting adequate sleep can have negative health consequences and can even exacerbate feelings of anxiety. Conversely, feeling anxious can result in sleep problems. This is sort of like the age-old question: "Which came first, the chicken or the egg?" Either way, this connection between sleep and anxiety speaks to the importance of getting a good night's sleep. Many of the exercises throughout this book can help you sleep more soundly if anxiety-inducing thoughts are keeping you up at night. A relaxing bath, of course, is a wonderful way to prepare to turn in for the night. Couple that with a mood-relaxing cup of herbal tea and a lavender sachet under your pillow, and a good night's sleep is even more likely.

dilute the oil in a carrier oil, such as almond oil. Essential oils can be found in pure form as well as in lotions, bath crystals, soap, and massage oils.

HERBAL TINCTURES Similar to essential oils, herbal tinctures are derived from various herbs that have been distilled in water or alcohol. The liquid extracts of an herb can be taken orally directly under the tongue or dropped into tea or water. They are commonly available in a bottle with a dropper that allows easy dispensing of just a few drops at a time.

SACHETS Dried herbs often retain their strong scents and healing qualities. Placing the herbs in a sachet, or a cloth bag, is a convenient way to use them. Sachets vary in size and the scents vary in strength. An herbal sachet can be used in a variety of ways, such as slipped into a pillowcase, placed in a closet or drawer, or carried around in a bag.

SUPPLEMENTS Your local health food store or vitamin shop probably has a number of supplements on its shelves that may help relieve the symptoms of anxiety. Many people turn to these natural remedies for support, and some prove helpful. However, each of us is unique and what works for one may not work for another. Be sure to consult with a health-care professional when considering supplements. Vitamin B, in particular, is important for brain function. A deficiency in this vitamin has been shown to result in nervousness, fatigue, and irritability. This is just one example, however. There is a plethora of information on the topic of supplements, so be sure to do your research.

Using Oils, Tinctures, and Herbs

Essential oils for everyday use generally come in small bottles that can be carried in your purse or satchel. Small tubes of essential oils can even be attached to a keychain or worn around your neck. If you find yourself in the midst of a stressful moment, you can take a moment to breathe in a relaxing scent. Simply place a few drops of diluted oil on your wrist or inhale directly from the bottle.

If you're wondering which essential oils might help you manage your anxiety, the following are a few that are recommended on the American College of Healthcare Sciences (ACHS) Health and Wellness Blog:

Essential Oils for Soothing the Soul

BERGAMOT (*CITRUS AURANTIUM* VAR. *CITRUS BERGAMIA*) Use this citrus-based oil when you want to lift your spirits. Essential oil of bergamot has been shown to be most effective for combating depression and anxiety, as reported by the ACHS article.

CLARY SAGE (*SALVIA SCLAREA*) Inhaling this oil is good for helping to "clear away" a negative mood. It's been known to reduce stress, depression, and anxiety.

LAVENDER (*LAVANDULA ANGUSTIFOLIA*) The scent of lavender has long been known to have relaxing effects, but studies have also shown that lavender can improve symptoms of depression and reduce levels of cortisol (the "stress hormone").

Like essential oils, tinctures can also be carried in your bag throughout the day or stored in a nearby cabinet or drawer. Due to their concentrated content, tinctures usually come in small, convenient bottles. This also makes a tincture easy to use on the go. Often, a few drops of the tincture are added to a glass of water, placed in a soothing cup of tea, or dropped directly under the tongue to allow it to more efficiently enter the bloodstream.

Dried herbs are also beneficial for their "aromatherapeutic" qualities. You can place sachets of healing herbs around your home or office in areas where you feel you could benefit most from the calming scents. Some people use aromatic eye masks to help themselves calm down at the end of a stressful day or place a small sachet of dried lavender near their bedside. Find a spot at your desk where you can tuck a sachet of calming herbs so that you can enjoy the benefits while you're working. You can also place sachets in your dresser drawers and carry the scent with you throughout the day on your clothing.

If You Only Have 5 Minutes
INHALE A CALMING SCENT

Find a quiet place where you can spend a few minutes inhaling a calming scent with your eyes closed. A couple good choices include those listed earlier diluted in a carrier oil. You may find other scents more relaxing or appealing. Test several before deciding upon one, and also be sure that you don't have a skin reaction if you apply the oil topically. Also be sure not to use synthetic scents for this purpose, as the synthetic chemicals may cause a headache.

1. Find a space where you feel removed from the environment that's causing you stress. For example, if you are at work, go to an empty conference room or the restroom, and bring the essential oil with you.

2. Close your eyes and take a few deep, cleansing breaths.

3. Place a few drops of the diluted oil on your wrist or neck. Be purposeful as you smooth the oil into your skin.

4. Deeply breathe in the calming scent, and imagine that the scent is flowing through your entire body, reaching each muscle and giving it a gentle, relaxing massage.

5. Carry this scent with you as you return to the environment that had been causing your anxiety. If you feel your anxiety rising once again, breathe in the scent, trying to remain anchored in its soothing aroma.

How do you feel after taking a few minutes to enjoy a soothing scent? Do you feel calmer? If one type of oil doesn't seem to have the desired effect, choose another until you find one that you can turn to in times of stress. You may also find that a combination of oils is just what you need to experience the benefits.

Natural Remedies Though History

Natural remedies have been used throughout the millennia for various health-related purposes and, in many cases, with good outcomes. A written record of the use of natural remedies dates back to ancient China when the principles of the healing methods were rooted in the theory that each human being is made up of five elements: fire, earth, water, wood, and metal. These days, the herbs used in traditional Chinese medicine (TCM) reflect these five elements and are used by TCM practitioners to effectuate harmony within a patient who is feeling imbalanced.

One of the most readily available and best-known natural remedies for relaxation is lavender. Ancient Romans and Greeks commonly used lavender to scent their bathwater. It was also used as a lice and flea remedy and was a popular masking agent used to improve the scent of streets and homes.

Another popular oil, bergamot, was used in the 1600s and 1700s in teas and perfumery. It was a common remedy for fevers throughout the sixteenth century.

When it comes to lemon balm, a member of the mint family, the University of Maryland Medical Center states on its website that this herb was used in the Middle Ages as a remedy to reduce anxiety, improve sleep and appetite, and ease indigestion. Looking even farther back, lemon balm also has a history of being a "spirit-booster" when added to wine and was used as a treatment for insect bites and stings.

Oftentimes, when selecting a natural remedy, its history of therapeutic use can be researched with little effort on the Internet or in books on natural remedies. When doing this type of research, always consider the source of the information to be sure it's reputable.

Natural Remedies: Help for Anxiety-Related Digestive Disorders

According to the ADAA and other sources, there is a correlation between anxiety disorders and irritable bowel syndrome (IBS), which is a disorder of the large intestines. Symptoms of IBS include pain, bloating, gas, cramping, diarrhea, and constipation. The colon (another name for the large intestines) is controlled by the nervous system, which is affected by stress and anxiety. Symptoms in the gastrointestinal tract can sometimes communicate anxiety-related information to us before we're even aware of what we're worried about. For example, you may wake up in the morning with a slight stomachache and wonder if you ate something spoiled the night before. Then, you remember that you're expecting a call from an important person, and you're nervous about the upcoming conversation. Although you weren't consciously thinking about the phone call when you woke up, it seems that your body was reminding you.

According to the ADAA, approximately one in five adults in the United States has IBS. Furthermore, the ADAA states that approximately 50 to 90 percent of patients who seek treatment for IBS also have a disorder such as anxiety or depression. If you suffer from IBS, you may be interested in learning about natural remedies that can ease your symptoms to supplement any medical steps you and your doctor are taking. Here are a few:

Natural Remedies for IBS

MINT Mint has long been a natural remedy for an upset stomach. Smelling or tasting mint activates enzymes that aid digestion.

GINGER Ginger promotes a natural rhythm of digestion by helping to regulate blood sugar levels. This herb is often used to alleviate symptoms of diarrhea.

If You Only Have 10 Minutes
SIP A CALMING TEA

In 2014, in the article "The World's Top Drink," *National Geographic* revealed that the most popular drink in the world is tea. While you might have assumed the world prefers coffee or cola, tea beat out the competition due to its accessibility, healing qualities, and long history of use. Even if you don't indulge in tea for the health benefits, nothing beats a warm cup of tea on a drizzly day for lifting your spirits. Try the calming tea below and enjoy the soothing scents and tastes.

CALMING CHAMOMILE TEA

SERVES 1 / PREP TIME: 5 MINUTES

1 bag chamomile tea
1 lemon wedge
1 tablespoon raw honey
Freshly grated ginger (to taste)

1. Brew a cup of the chamomile tea according to package directions.
2. Squeeze lemon into the tea.
3. Stir in raw honey.
4. Add grated ginger to taste.
5. Drop in lemon wedge, if desired.
6. Drink and enjoy!

Consider making two servings of tea, and share a cup with someone you care about. The relaxing qualities of the tea can encourage deep conversations that may leave you feeling supported and heard, which can further reduce your anxiety.

FIBER Dietary fiber, such as whole-grain products, can relieve symptoms of constipation and aid in digestion.

SMALLER MEALS Large meals require more work from the digestive tract, which can exacerbate IBS symptoms. Therefore, it's been suggested that people with IBS eat smaller meals throughout the day rather than the standard three large meals.

DIETARY RESTRICTIONS Some health-care professionals recommend that people with IBS avoid dairy products, acid-forming foods, and carbonated beverages, as these foods may worsen IBS symptoms.

Nature is amazing. Oftentimes, it has everything we need to help us feel better and happier. But like everything in life, there are positives and negatives to nature's offerings. Keep in mind that just because something comes from nature doesn't mean there will be no side effects related to its use. So, when considering natural remedies, always consult a health-care professional for guidance.

If You Have 30 Minutes

TAKE A CALMING BATH

If you've had a particularly anxiety-inducing day, treat yourself to a warm, relaxing bath that allows you to engage your senses with the addition of your chosen anxiety-relieving essential oil. (As you've learned, lavender was often used in Greek and Roman baths, so you may want to give that oil a try.) Engaging your senses is a good way to draw your mind away from negative thoughts and into a more positive place where you can practice your mindfulness skills and simply appreciate the moment.

1. Fill your bathtub with warm water—not too hot and not too cold. Place several drops of the essential oil into the water.

2. Dim the artificial lights and light a candle or two to provide natural soft light. Sink down into the bath, inhaling the aroma.

3. As you relax in the water, take a few minutes to be grateful for this opportunity to take time for yourself.

4. Practice being mindful and breathe deeply with your full attention on your breath. You may choose to meditate or simply just relax until the water begins to feel cool.

When bath time is over, how do you feel? Do you feel more relaxed? Did you enjoy the calming scent? It's often beneficial to take a calming bath before going to bed. With your muscles loosened and your thoughts quieted, a restful night's sleep is more likely. And when you have a restful night's sleep, you might discover that the next day runs a little more smoothly.

Diet and Exercise

A good diet and regular exercise are essential additions to anyone's health-care regimen, but they can be especially important when dealing with social anxiety. Keep in mind that social anxiety can often lead to feelings of fatigue or low energy, because repetitive negative thoughts and avoidant behaviors can feel exhausting. If you're feeling less than energetic due to your experiences with social anxiety, it might feel like a challenge to even imagine incorporating physical activity or a healthy diet into your daily routine. Remember that you only have to start—just start.

At first, don't worry about running a specific distance or eating a certain number of servings of vegetables each day. Simply get moving, eat one healthy snack, and feel proud of yourself for taking that first step toward health. It's easy to look at the big picture and feel overwhelmed. You may find yourself thinking things such as: *What's the point of even starting? I'll never be able to run five miles.* Instead, acknowledge that you have to start somewhere and you'd rather feel proud for trying than regret not taking a chance. You could tell yourself, *I'll walk for 20 minutes today. Maybe I'll pick up the pace and jog for a few of those minutes.* Much like other approaches to alleviating social anxiety, there will be periods of trial and error; take your time to find out what works for you.

QUICK QUIZ

You wake up on a Saturday morning, and you have two choices: Join your friend at the gym for the beginner's aerobic class she invited you to last week or stay at home to relax after a stressful week at work. When you agreed to take the aerobics class, it sounded like a great idea, but now you're worried that you won't be able to keep up with the class, you don't have the right workout outfit, you don't feel energized or motivated, and you don't have a gym membership so you'll have to stop at the front desk for a visitor's pass. All of these thoughts are causing your anxiety levels to rise. You wonder why the simple idea of going to the gym to get some exercise makes you quake inside. Do you:

A. Call your friend and make up an excuse, such as you're not feeling well, to get out of going, and then do your normal Saturday routine that doesn't include any physical activity other than maybe some light housework or gardening?

B. Tell your friend that you just don't feel comfortable going, but decide to do some light stretching and maybe take a long walk or bike ride instead?

C. Put on your workout clothes and do a few simple stretches to get yourself limbered up and a few jumping jacks to get your blood pumping, then eat a healthy breakfast? A little while later, you get yourself over to gym, despite your anxiety over the new situation.

D. Don't even consider staying at home because you're excited about starting a new exercise routine, and this beginner's aerobics class is probably going to be a great start? You get there early because you know you have to sign up for a visitor's pass, reminding yourself that the person at the front desk is there to help you.

Starting an exercise routine can feel daunting at first, but you know that being active comes with a whole array of benefits. If you selected A, chances are you're letting your anxiety dictate what you're going to do, and the information in this chapter will help you put activity above your concerns. If you selected B, you're still letting your anxiety control your actions, but at least you know how important it is to get active, and you'll take steps to do so. If you selected C or D, there's a good chance you've been practicing the exercises in this book, and you're ready to take on the new challenge. Good for you! This is a challenge you'll be glad you took.

Get Physical

Even people who don't struggle with social anxiety say regular exercise helps reduce their stress levels and keeps them centered. Exercise jump-starts your body into creating more serotonin and endorphins ("feel-good" hormones) in your brain. When you looked at the ways that anxiety affects your brain earlier in the book, you saw that an anxious brain often produces lower amounts of serotonin or has trouble absorbing the chemical. Remember, serotonin is the neurotransmitter that affects mood. If exercise naturally increases the amount of serotonin in the brain, it makes sense to incorporate more exercise into your daily life.

Another benefit of physical exercise is the opportunity to work out with friends, family, or acquaintances. When you engage in exercise with friends, as part of a group or a program, you'll also strengthen your social network and support system. You may notice a rise in self-esteem and confidence by participating in an activity that not only helps you lead a healthier lifestyle, but also connects you to the outside world.

The US Department of Health and Human Services recommends 30 minutes of moderate exercise daily; however, if you're just starting out, begin with shorter increments of time with lower-intensity physical activity. Regardless of how you choose to approach a new exercise routine, always check in with a health-care professional before starting.

Anxiety and the Heart

One of the first signs of anxiety is often an increased heart rate. While this may seem like an acute symptom without any long-term consequences, there is a clear link between the health of your heart and the frequency of your anxiety. For example, studies that involved Harvard Medical School and the Lown Cardiovascular Research Foundation, as well as a study done by several Canadian medical colleges, found evidence that anxiety disorders increase the likelihood of suffering a heart attack. When looking at both men and women who have suffered heart attacks, those living with an anxiety disorder were twice as likely to experience a heart attack.

If You Only Have 5 Minutes
STRETCH YOUR BODY

When you feel your anxiety increasing and you want to get back on track as soon as possible, spend five minutes stretching. You can perform this exercise in your office, at home, or anywhere you'll have a few minutes of privacy. The goal of the activity is to calm you and help you feel more balanced emotionally, physically, and mentally. Follow these steps:

1. Plant your feet hip-width apart and imagine that your feet are rooted into the earth.

2. Inhale deeply while sweeping your arms skyward and reach them above your head. Feel your body stretching its entire length.

3. As you exhale, fold at your midsection and reach your hands toward the earth. Feel the stretch along your spine and back muscles and behind your knees.

4. Return to a normal standing position and take three deep breaths.

5. Repeat steps 2 and 3 at least two more times with a focus on engaging your breath with your movements.

This brief exercise in movement and breathing can help you realign your energy with your physical being. How did stretching make you feel? How did it affect your thinking process, your heart rate, and your emotions? Regardless of the physical activity you choose, be sure to analyze its benefits to your overall well-being by asking yourself these questions immediately following the activity.

This is a sobering discovery for anyone living with social anxiety and should be taken into consideration when trying to find an exercise regimen that will work for you. Physical exercise is encouraged in people with anxiety not only to decrease the symptoms of anxiety, but also to improve overall heart health.

There are many different types of exercise to choose from that will not only help quiet and clear your mind, but also get your heart working more efficiently. Consider combining mindful movements with more strenuous aerobic exercises.

Mindful Movement

Various forms of physical exercise can help support a better quality of life, but certain types can also help you develop a stronger connection between your mind and body. Combining several mindful activities with aerobic activities is an excellent approach to overall fitness of body and mind. Take a look at the following examples of physical activities that calm the mind while working the body to see if any sound appealing to you.

Common Mindful Physical Activities

YOGA Yoga is an approach to exercise that combines the quieting of the mind with fluid motions of the body. It helps you strengthen and lengthen your muscles while also controlling your mind and breath with each movement. Yoga incorporates many of the same techniques found in mindfulness and breathing exercises.

TAI CHI Rooted in ancient China, tai chi helps you reduce stress through fluid, graceful movements that are executed with focus and deep breathing. Tai chi maintains constant, smooth movement of the body, helping you feel connected to every muscle.

PILATES Pilates embraces similar philosophies of yoga, but it is designed to help strengthen your muscles, particularly those in your midsection known as your core muscles. Pilates allows you to focus on specific muscles and build strength over time, while also promoting more balance in your everyday life.

DANCING Fast dancing gets your heart rate up and can increase your feel-good emotions, getting you more in touch with the positive aspects of yourself. Moving your body to the rhythm of music is an intimate experience, whether dancing alone, in a group, or with a partner.

The goal of mindful physical activities is to engage your body in thoughtful, purposeful movements that have the power to help you control your anxiety. You might consider pacing each movement to match your breath or timing each movement to accompany a positive affirmation. Because social anxiety has a tendency to make people feel disconnected from their feelings (with the exception of fear, anxiety, and other uncomfortable emotions), mindful activities can help create a more positive connection.

Aerobic Exercise

Exercise increases your heart rate and strengthens your heart's ability to pump more blood throughout your body. When your muscles have more oxygen-rich blood being fed into them, the stronger they will become and the healthier you will be. How will you know if your activity is raising your heart rate to the level it should be? The Centers for Disease Control and Prevention (CDC) explains how to determine your target heart rate on its website (see the resources section). Your health-care professional or a certified personal trainer at the gym can guide you in the right direction as well. In general, when you have achieved your target heart rate, you'll still be able to talk during exercise, but you won't be able to sing along to your favorite song.

For some ideas of aerobic exercises—some of which you can do while listening to music—check out these examples:

- Running
- Fast-walking
- Swimming
- Biking
- Tennis
- Basketball
- Hiking
- Rock-climbing

Pause for a moment to think of physical activities you know you already enjoy or used to enjoy. How often do you engage in these activities? Do you think there's a way to incorporate them more often into your daily routine? Next, consider forms of exercise you want to try, but haven't yet. Think seasonally. Maybe summer is coming up and you've always wanted to try kayaking. Or maybe you live in an area that's known for its snowy winters and you've thought about giving snowshoeing a whirl.

When looking for ways to fill your life with more exercise, seek comfort and variety. It's always great to hone the skills of an activity you're familiar with, but the more variety you're able to incorporate into your routine, the better. Variety will engage muscles you aren't used to working and will test your strength in new ways. Look at it as a chance to be proud of yourself for trying something new.

If You Only Have 10 Minutes

WALK OFF YOUR ANXIETY

When your anxiety or stressful feelings are starting to build, take 10 minutes to get back on track. If you work at a desk all day long, bring a pair of walking shoes to the office with you. You might even consider leaving a pair at the office so that they're readily available whenever you feel the need to walk off your anxiety. Whether it's a timed break at the office or a brief window of time during another part of the day, slip into your comfortable shoes and take these steps:

1. Go outside and begin walking at a brisk pace.
2. Use this time to get your heart rate up and mindfully observe the world around you. Take note of the people you pass, the weather, and anything else that captures your attention.
3. As you walk, take deep, cleansing breaths and appreciate the fresh air filling your lungs.
4. Walk for five minutes and then head back. Keep your attention on the scenery. Notice how it looks different from before with this reversed perspective. Slow your pace the closer you get to your starting point and allow your heart rate to settle down.
5. Upon returning to your original starting point, take a few minutes to evaluate how you feel.

Set an intention to use a few of your breaks at work to get outside and enjoy this activity. You may even decide to extend your walking time or try a more exerting activity another time.

General Health Benefits of Exercise

According to the CDC, in addition to helping reduce anxiety, regular exercise has many health benefits. To better understand how exercise can improve your overall health, read the following:

REDUCES THE RISK OF CERTAIN CANCERS Research shows that people who are physically active show a lower risk of breast cancer and colon cancer than those people who are not physically active.

REDUCES THE RISK OF CARDIOVASCULAR DISEASE Heart disease is one of the leading causes of death in the United States. With regular moderate-intensity physical activity, you can lower your blood pressure and cholesterol levels, thereby improving heart health.

REDUCES THE RISK OF TYPE-2 DIABETES AND METABOLIC SYNDROME As you may know, type-2 diabetes is a condition that affects the way the body processes sugar. Metabolic syndrome, a lesser-known condition, is a cluster of abnormalities that increases the risk of heart disease, stroke, and diabetes. People who exercise for 2–2.5 hours each week show lower levels of blood pressure, cholesterol, blood sugar, and triglycerides, all of which in high levels can lead to metabolic syndrome.

The above benefits don't include the psychological benefits you'll gain from incorporating exercise into your daily routine, as discussed earlier. That's an important one to keep in mind! However, a reduced risk of major disease is good motivation as well. If you aren't feeling motivated to get started, consider these reasons to get you moving.

A Balanced Diet

For some people, eating can be used as a way to avoid or relieve feelings of anxiety. Oftentimes, the food turned to might be considered comfort food, which is generally less healthy. If you eat comfort food or junk food, you might feel good in the moment, but the feeling isn't as long lasting as you'd probably like it to be. Research supports that maintaining a *good* diet can directly improve your general mood. There's no need to turn to junk food to do the trick.

A study published in *The American Journal of Psychiatry* in 2010 assessed the dietary habits of approximately 1,000 women. Researchers found that a diet composed of vegetables, fruit, beef, lamb, fish, and whole grains was associated with a lower likelihood of depressive and anxiety disorders. Of course it's important to keep in mind that every individual case is different. There are always other factors that will influence one's mood, such as socioeconomic status, additional health challenges, and environmental factors. Nevertheless, improving your diet to include more healthy options is a low-risk way to help improve your quality of life.

When your social anxiety starts to feel like it's taking over your day, bringing your focus back to something as simple and approachable as what you're going to eat at your next meal can help diminish your anxiety. Sometimes even the act of cooking a meal can alleviate stress.

QUICK QUIZ

Imagine you've just picked up your two kids from band practice, and they're complaining about being hungry. You've just come from work where you had a particularly anxiety-inducing meeting, and your nerves are already on edge. You're tired, frustrated, and feel a headache building as the kids continue to complain. As it turns out, you're hungry, too. Do you:

A. Call your significant other to ask if he or she would mind dealing with dinner tonight and leave it up to your partner to choose what's served?

B. Pull into a fast-food drive-thru and order easy, tasty food for everyone?

C. Calmly observe your anxiety and ask your kids what they want to eat for dinner? If they suggest something unhealthy, you decide it will be okay "just for tonight."

D. Observe your anxiety from a distance and brainstorm with your kids what you could prepare for dinner that would be both healthy and tasty? Then you all stop at the grocery store and go on a "scavenger hunt" to gather the ingredients you'll use to make dinner when you get home.

You may find that your anxiety prompts you to reach for the easiest solution to resolve hunger, which is often not the healthiest solution. When your decision-making includes other people, you might be even more inclined to find a quicker solution, despite its nutritional value. If you selected A, B, or C, you're probably familiar with the habit of leaning toward what's more comfortable. However, a little extra time and effort can make a world of difference on your physical and mental health.

Practicing Mindfulness While Cooking

Mindfully preparing and eating food is a practice you can easily incorporate into your everyday life. As in the previous example, you might be used to reaching for something quick and easy. You might also look at food preparation as just another time-consuming chore. However, when you make preparing your meals a mindful task, you'll find that this is an excellent everyday opportunity to help you increase your positive thoughts while taking steps to nourish your body.

Instead of going over a laundry list of to-dos as you prepare dinner, be fully present in the moment. The preparation and enjoyment of food can be a sensual experience that connects you with your own humanity. The body needs fuel not only to survive, but also to thrive. Use these moments to appreciate the access you have to healthy food and your ability to prepare your meals how you like them.

As you prepare the food, pay close attention to the smells of the various ingredients. Notice the varied colors. How does the ingredient feel? Is it sticky, hard, soft, wet, dry, or something else? Does it slice easily? When you combine two ingredients, does their appearance change? Do you notice anything new about the aroma or consistency? Be thoughtful in every action you take while preparing your meal. This will help you practice mindfulness during your daily activities, while encouraging you to be more conscious of what you're putting into your body.

Foods to Keep You Balanced

Think about what you ate this past week for breakfast, lunch, and dinner. Try to remember as much as you can, even jotting it down if that helps. When you look over your typical "meal plan," you might discover that you've been eating the same foods every day and possibly even that they don't represent a balanced diet. Due to the hurried nature of everyday life, you may find it easier to grab a quick pastry from the office lounge, call in a to-go order from the hamburger place downstairs, or eat an energy bar as a dinner replacement. However, if you want to help manage your social anxiety through healthy eating, add some of the following balancing foods to your grocery list:

Balancing Foods

COMPLEX CARBOHYDRATES Whole grains, such as whole-grain breads, whole-grain cereals, quinoa, and oatmeal. Complex carbohydrates may increase your serotonin levels.

TRYPTOPHAN-RICH FOODS Eggs, turkey, bananas, oysters, clams, nuts, seeds, and milk, among others. These foods contain the amino acid tryptophan, which affects the body's synthesis of serotonin.

WATER It's vitally important to remain hydrated, whether or not you experience anxiety. Be aware, however, that even low levels of dehydration can negatively affect a person's mood.

FOODS RICH IN HEALTHY FATS Healthy fats include monounsaturated fat and polyunsaturated fat, such as omega-3 fatty acids. Healthy fats are found in nuts such as walnuts, seeds such as flaxseeds, olive oil, avocados, and salmon, among others. Foods high in healthy fats have been shown to improve blood cholesterol levels and reduce the risk of heart disease.

If You Only Have 10 Minutes

HAVE A STRESS-REDUCING SMOOTHIE

If you're looking for a good anxiety-reducing meal you can take on the go, whip yourself up a smoothie full of calming, wholesome ingredients! Try the following recipe or experiment with the ingredients you have handy.

STRESS-REDUCING SMOOTHIE

SERVES 1 / PREP TIME: 10 MINUTES

1 cup ice (more or less, depending on preference)
1 banana, peeled and sliced into 1-inch pieces
1 handful fresh blueberries (or frozen, if fresh unavailable)
4 ounces fresh pineapple chunks (or canned, if fresh unavailable)
1 tablespoon raw honey
Almond milk or soymilk (if desired)

1. Crush ice in blender.
2. Add banana, blueberries, and pineapple, and blend until smooth.
3. Add honey and blend again.
4. If desired, add milk and blend until smoothie reaches desired consistency.
5. Pour into a large glass or travel cup and enjoy!

When you choose to eat fruit and other good-for-you foods, you're affirming that you value your health. If you feel anxiety building up, remind yourself of your choice to have a healthy meal, which means you're on the path to a healthier life.

VITAMIN C–RICH FOODS Citrus fruits and tomatoes are high in vitamin C, which can aid in lowering levels of the stress hormone cortisol.

FOODS RICH IN OTHER VITAMINS AND MINERALS Fresh fruits, vegetables, herbs, and spices. Different plant foods contain different vitamins and minerals, all of which are necessary for good health.

Alcohol Use and the Anxious Mind

Some people living with social anxiety may find themselves turning to alcohol as a method of calming their nerves in a social setting. However, it's important to be aware that according to the ADAA, approximately 20 percent of people who struggle with social anxiety also suffer from alcohol abuse or dependence.

It's understandable that socially anxious people might want to use alcohol to help soothe their anxiety or escape the uncomfortable symptoms. Alcohol can temporarily reduce the symptoms of anxiety, providing a sense of calm and relaxation. You might enjoy feeling less inhibited and more confident when you drink. The downside, however, is that only a few hours after drinking and/or the following day, you may experience an increase in irritability, depression, or anxiety.

To better understand the warning signs of alcoholism, take a moment to observe the following list of behaviors compiled by the ADAA. If you engage in at least one of the following, you might have formed an addiction to alcohol:

- Drink alcohol four or more times a week

- Have five or more alcoholic drinks in one day

- Not be able to stop drinking once you've started

(30) If You Have 30 Minutes
PREPARE A WELL-BALANCED MEAL

Set aside some time to prepare yourself a balanced, calming meal. Each of the ingredients below has been carefully selected to provide you with the healthiest, most flavorful meal that can also help alleviate your anxiety. These recipes incorporate the healthy foods discussed earlier.

SIMPLE SALMON

SERVES 1 / PREP TIME: 10 MINUTES

6 ounces fresh salmon, skin removed
2 tablespoons butter
1 tablespoon garlic powder
Salt and pepper to taste, if desired
1 lemon wedge

1. Evenly coat salmon with garlic powder.
2. Melt butter in a skillet over medium heat.
3. Place salmon in skillet and cook for approximately 5 minutes on each side until the fish is flaky and lightly browned.
4. Remove salmon from the skillet. Season to taste. Squeeze lemon over the fish.
5. Serve alongside quinoa salad.

QUINOA SALAD

SERVES 3 / PREP TIME: 25 MINUTES

1 cup dry quinoa

2 medium avocados, peeled and pits removed

1 large fresh tomato or a few handfuls of cherry tomatoes

2 tablespoons balsamic vinegar

2 tablespoons olive oil

1 tablespoon garlic powder

Salt and pepper to taste

1. Cook the quinoa according to package directions and transfer to a medium-sized bowl to cool.
2. Dice the avocado flesh into 1-inch cubes.
3. Chop the tomato into 1-inch cubes or slice cherry tomatoes in half.
4. Combine the balsamic vinegar, olive oil, garlic powder, pepper, and salt in a separate bowl.
5. Gently toss avocado and tomato into the cooled quinoa.
6. Drizzle the oil–vinegar mixture over the quinoa, and stir gently until thoroughly combined.
7. Enjoy a single serving along with your salmon.

There's enough quinoa salad to go around, but consider making an extra serving of the salmon and sharing it with someone you care about. Sharing a meal is an excellent opportunity to deepen your connection with a friend or family member. The act of showing gratitude to someone through the gift of a delicious meal will leave both of you feeling fulfilled and valued.

- Need a drink in the morning to get yourself going
- Feel guilty or remorseful after drinking
- Have had a relative, friend, coworker, or doctor express concern about your use of alcohol

If you're coping with social anxiety by using alcohol, seek help. A dependency can gradually develop over time without you even realizing it. The more alcohol you consume, the higher your tolerance becomes, which then requires greater consumption to achieve the same calming effect.

Dependency on alcohol isn't something to be ashamed about. There are many people who have fought the same battle and feel the way you feel. There are compassionate health-care professionals who understand this dependency, are trained to help you understand how and why you choose to cope with alcohol, and provide you with tools and support. Be kind and compassionate with yourself, and give yourself the gift of healing.

Your everyday obligations probably take up a lot of your time, but if you want to experience the anxiety-relieving benefits of exercise and smart eating, you'll find moments throughout your day to incorporate healthy habits in the form of physical activity and a more-balanced diet into your life. Part of regaining control of your life from social anxiety is making choices that will benefit your health. Choose to bring your awareness to how to engage in the world with your physical body. Try to identify if your exercise habits and dietary habits could use any improvement and then challenge yourself to simply start—just start.

Continuing the Process

As you reach the end of this book, you might be wondering what your next steps will be. Perhaps you found the exercises helpful for taking the initial steps to relieve your social anxiety, but you feel as if you could benefit even further if you began to attend regular therapy sessions and/or joined a support group. Keep in mind that intent and action are different—if you feel you could use the help of a therapist or support group, be sure to follow through with action. Also make an intention to continue the process of learning how to manage your social anxiety—in whatever direction that takes you. Follow the path one step at a time, and your goal will be within reach.

Seeking Outside Support

How do you feel when you think about seeing a therapist or joining a support group? Identify any concerns you might have. Are
you concerned what other people will think? Are you concerned
that your job would be on the line if someone from your company
discovered you were attending a support group or 12-step program? Are you afraid of exposing your insecurities and fears to
another person, even if he or she is trained to help you? People
often avoid seeking help for longer than is necessary because
they can feel trapped in their fears and insecurities. Pay attention
to your thoughts concerning professional help and, using what
you learned about observing your thoughts in Chapter 4, assess
whether or not they are realistic. Replace any unhelpful thoughts
with helpful ones.

Whether you're seeking a therapist to assist you with exposure
therapy, CBT, talk therapy, or something else, make an action plan
for yourself and then hold yourself accountable. As stated at the
beginning of this book, the most important thing is being committed to improving your health and not giving up. Don't be afraid to
ask for help. If you aren't quite sure where to start, spend some time
reviewing the resources section at the end of this book. You can
also contact the clinician who initially diagnosed you with SAD for
helpful leads.

Joining a Support Group

One of the best ways to process your experiences with social anxiety is to join a SAD support group. The benefits of spending time with others who are having similar experiences include an increased sense of self and community, support, encouragement, and a deep feeling of being heard and understood. In a support group, the idea is to openly and candidly talk about what you're going through, including your setbacks or triumphs. When you attend a support group, you can share your personal goals and help others pursue theirs. Let's take a look at one last example:

Samuel, age 62, from Charlotte, North Carolina, has struggled with social anxiety his entire life. He recalls his anxiety starting when his family moved across the country for his father's job just as Samuel was completing elementary school. The anxiety increased over the years. He felt too embarrassed to tell anyone what he was going through. His father had raised him to be "strong." Any display of emotion or uncertainty was frowned upon, so he learned to hide how he truly felt and became withdrawn. His family, friends, and later even his wife and children, all thought of Samuel as "quiet" and "distant." He spent years avoiding anxiety-inducing situations and found himself feeling more and more isolated and alone. He wondered if anyone, including his wife, truly understood him.

Then, one of Samuel's children came home from college for the weekend and brought along his psychology textbook. As Samuel flipped through the book, he stumbled across a chapter on anxiety disorders. Reading about SAD, he recognized his own thoughts, feelings, and behaviors in the descriptions. He suddenly felt understood in a way he had rarely experienced. When he showed his wife the description of SAD, she encouraged him to seek help. Samuel ended up connecting with a local support group for people struggling with social anxiety. Within the first few meetings, Samuel began to feel understood, heard, and accepted. It allowed him to feel more comfortable opening up to his wife about how he felt in social situations, which resulted in a stronger relationship between them as well as a more fulfilling life.

As was the case with Samuel, the first step in seeking support begins the moment you realize you can benefit from having someone in your life who understands what you're going through. The ADAA website offers a searchable database for support groups by state. If you're thinking of joining a support group, this association's website would be a great place to start. (See the resources section.)

Your Personal Process of Self-Discovery

Now that you've read the sample scenarios and gained insight into the types of experiences people have while living with social anxiety, there's still one more story you need to spend time with: your own. Throughout these pages, you've been encouraged to examine your thoughts, feelings, habits, and behaviors. Some activities have asked you to test yourself, push yourself, and better understand yourself. You've even been asked to keep a journal to start looking at yourself more in depth and to track your progress. You've come a long way, but don't stop here. Continue this process of self-discovery and delve into your personal story as deeply as you can. You have embarked on a journey to better understand yourself and your social anxiety, so stay on course. Yes, it takes courage and strength to look at yourself with complete honesty, but it's the only way to truly start healing.

Hopefully, you've embraced the idea of keeping a journal. If you're still hesitant, however, keep in mind that a journal can look and feel however you think would be most beneficial to you. For example, some people may think of a journal as blank pages in a book to write on. In fact, there are journal pages for you to use at the end of this book. However, you can also keep a journal in a computer file or using the notes feature on your phone or tablet. You can also download a journal app to your device. Another idea is to keep an audio journal using a voice recorder. You might even want to create a video diary using the webcam on your computer.

Avoid the limiting idea that if you aren't a good writer, you can't keep a journal. Remember, this is for no one else's eyes but yours. It doesn't matter how well you write or even if you use complete sentences. Journaling is an excellent tool on your healing journey because the more you practice paying attention to your thoughts, the closer you'll come to managing your social anxiety. Remind yourself that it's important, and think outside the box.

Am I Cured Yet?

After reading this book, you might feel energized and ready to overcome your social anxiety. However, it's important to understand that SAD is often a lifelong condition, and being "cured" of it is an overstatement. Learn to work with your SAD—be stronger than it, but don't deny its presence. As discussed throughout, the fear of experiencing anxiety itself can trigger your anxiety. Don't be afraid of it. Learn to accept that SAD may always be part of your life, but it doesn't have to determine your quality of life. You can either be run by your social anxiety or choose how to run your social anxiety.

As you've journeyed through this book, you've learned about CBT, exposure therapy, mindfulness, meditation, diet, exercise, natural remedies, and practicing gratitude, among other strategies. With each new piece of knowledge you've gained, you've also been presented with exercises that you can do in 5, 10, or 30 minutes. If you ever feel like you don't have a lot of time, just flip open these pages and choose a simple five-minute exercise.

Take each strategy in turn. Try one, then try another, and soon you may come to a place where you can put all of them in your tool-kit. If you ever find yourself feeling overwhelmed by your anxiety, turn back to Chapter 7 and take five minutes to bring awareness to your breath. Or open up to Chapter 5 and practice mindfulness as you go about your daily routine.

Above all, remember to be gentle with yourself—don't force yourself if you aren't ready to try these exercises or treatments. Forcing yourself will only exacerbate your anxiety and leave you feeling discouraged. The purpose of this book and the exercises within are meant to encourage you to seek a more positive outlook on your life. If, at any moment, you feel an exercise may do more harm than good or if you find an idea too distressing, give yourself permission to step away. That's not to say that you won't feel challenged by activities outside your comfort zone. Feeling challenged is beneficial. Think of the discomfort as a form of growing pains. When you encourage yourself to try something new, expect there to be an adjustment period. Be patient, and growth will occur.

You possess all the positive qualities that a person without social anxiety possesses. You're capable of feeling deeply and displaying empathy. You deserve to feel safe and comfortable in social settings. The fact that you've read this book and taken steps to better understand yourself and your social anxiety is a sign of your strength and capability. If your social anxiety threatens to control your quality of life, take comfort in knowing you can open up this book or seek out other resources to take back the control. You *always* have the choice to learn more, try more, and discover more about social anxiety and how it affects you. Thank you for taking the time to read this book. More important, thank you for believing in yourself!

Appendix

SAMPLE DAILY SCHEDULES FOR MANAGING YOUR SOCIAL ANXIETY

1. When you wake up, practice the five-minute gratitude exercise in Chapter 8. Take a few moments to appreciate the abundance in your life to set a positive tone for the day ahead.

2. In the middle of the day, practice the 10-minute exercise in Chapter 4. This exercise asks you to write down your fears about an anxiety-inducing situation and then directly address each concern. Practice accepting that you aren't perfect.

3. In the early evening, spend a half hour engaging in one of the mindful physical activities, such as yoga, introduced in Chapter 12.

SAMPLE SCHEDULE #2

1. As you go about your usual morning routine, practice mindfulness (see the exercise in Chapter 5). Use this time to pay close attention to the sights, sounds, tastes, and smells of your routine. Try to see all your experiences with fresh eyes, bringing your attention into the present moment.

2. At some point during the day, choose to be bold. Encourage yourself to be "exposed" to something that usually triggers your anxiety, such as engaging coworkers in conversation, as discussed in Chapter 6. Take a small step, be present in the

moment until your anxiety fades, and then feel incredibly proud of yourself afterward.

3. Before turning in for the night, draw yourself a calming bath. Refer to the exercise outlined in Chapter 11. Place a few drops of lavender essential oil into the bathwater to create a soothing aromatic environment that can help melt away your anxiety.

SAMPLE SCHEDULE #3

1. Start your day off by engaging in a physical activity (see Chapter 12 for ideas). Maybe you feel like riding your bike or jogging around the neighborhood. Or perhaps you'll choose to do a set of jumping jacks in your bedroom. Whatever you choose, be sure the activity will get your heart rate up.

2. Give yourself the gift of quiet time at some point during the day to practice one of the meditation exercises discussed in Chapter 7. Find a comfortable place to stand or sit and "just be."

3. When you're finished working for the day, take some time to prepare a healthy meal that incorporates several of the anxiety-reducing ingredients listed in Chapter 12. Consider inviting a friend or family member to join you for the meal.

SAMPLE SCHEDULE #4

1. In the morning, place several drops of diluted essential oil on your wrist and neck. Breathe deeply and start your morning off with appreciation for the calming scent.

2. In the afternoon, step away from whatever you're doing and brew yourself a cup of calming, relaxing tea (see the recipe in Chapter 11).

3. At the end of the day, write about your experiences in your journal. You might want to track negative thought patterns as you

did in the exercise in Chapter 4 or you may decide to create a gratitude list as you did in Chapter 8. Take time to be introspective to better understand yourself and your anxiety.

SAMPLE SCHEDULE #5

1. Before you begin your morning routine, take a few moments to check in with yourself by paying attention to your breath. Return to Chapter 7 for a breathing exercise that helps quiet your mind.

2. If you encounter a situation in which you feel like your opinion isn't being heard, practice using your "I" statements as discussed in Chapter 9. Be sure to check in with yourself afterward to see how you feel. Although it might have been a scary experience, you're also reinforcing your self-worth by maturely sharing your opinion.

3. At the end of the day, compose a letter to someone you'd like to thank as discussed in Chapter 8. Think of a person who helped you, supported you, or simply listened to you. Express your gratitude to this person through the written word. You can hand deliver or mail the letter the next day.

Additional Resources

Alcoholics Anonymous
475 Riverside Drive at West 120th St., 11th Floor
New York, NY 10115
(212) 870-3400
www.aa.org

Anxiety and Depression Association of America
8701 Georgia Avenue, Suite #412
Silver Spring, MD 20910
(204) 485-1001
www.adaa.org

Association for Behavioral and Cognitive Therapies
305 7th Avenue, 16th Floor
New York, NY 10001
(212) 647-1890
www.abct.org/home/

The Beck Institute for Cognitive Behavior Therapy
One Belmont Avenue, Suite 700
Bala Cynwood, PA 19004
(610) 664-3020
www.beckinstitute.org

Centers for Disease Control and Prevention
1600 Clifton Road
Atlanta, GA 30329
(800) 232-4636
www.cdc.gov

The Greater Good Science Center
University of California, Berkeley, MC 6070
Berkeley, CA 94720
(510) 642-2490
www.greatergood.berkeley.edu

International Foundation for Functional
Gastrointestinal Disorders
700 W. Virginia Street, #201
Milwaukee, WI 53204
(414) 964-1799
www.aboutibs.org

The Mindfulness Solution
c/o Ronald D. Siegel, PsyD
20 Longmeadow Road
Lincoln, MA 01773
781-259-3434
www.mindfulness-solution.com

Social Anxiety Institute
North Park, San Diego, CA 92104
(619) 272-2526
https://socialanxietyinstitute.org

References

American Medical Student Association. "Health Hint: Breathing Exercises." Accessed April 20, 2015. www.amsa.org/healingthehealer/breathing.cfm.

American Psychiatric Association. *Diagnostic and Statistical Manual of Mental Disorders*, 5th Edition (DSM-5). Washington, DC: American Psychiatric Association, 2013.

Anxiety and Depression Association of America, ADAA. "Facts & Statistics." Accessed May 14, 2015. www.adaa.org/about-adaa/press-room/facts-statistics.

Anxiety and Depression Association of America, ADAA. "Irritable Bowel Syndrome (IBS)." Accessed May 6, 2015. www.adaa.org/understanding-anxiety/related-illnesses/irritable-bowel-syndrome-ibs.

Anxiety and Depression Association of America, ADAA. "Medication." Accessed April 10, 2015. www.adaa.org/finding-help/treatment/medication.

Anxiety and Depression Association of America, ADAA. "Panic Disorders & Agoraphobia/Symptoms." Accessed May 6, 2015. www.adaa.org/understanding-anxiety/panic-disorder-agoraphobia/symptoms.

Anxiety and Depression Association of America, ADAA. "Sleep Disorders." Accessed May 6, 2015. www.adaa.org/understanding-anxiety/related-illnesses/sleep-disorders.

Anxiety and Depression Association of America, ADAA. "Social Anxiety Disorder." Accessed May 14, 2015. www.adaa.org/understanding-anxiety/social-anxiety-disorder.

Beck Institute of Cognitive Behavioral Therapy. "History of Cognitive Therapy." Accessed April 10, 2015. www.beckinstitute.org/history-of-cbt/.

Benson, Etienne. "The Many Faces of Perfectionism: The Need for Perfection Comes in Different Flavors, Each Associated With its Own Set of Problems, Researchers Say." American Psychological Association. November 2003. Accessed April 18, 2015. www.apa.org/monitor/nov03/manyfaces.aspx.

Bergamot Oil. "Unveiling Its Past—Bergamot Essential Oil." Bergamot Oil. June 1, 2012. Accessed April 19, 2015. www.bergamot-oil.com/category/history-and-origin.

Bergland, Christopher. "How Does Meditation Reduce Anxiety at a Neural Level?" Psychology Today. June 07, 2013. Accessed April 11, 2015. www.psychologytoday.com/blog/the-athletes-way/201306/how-does-meditation-reduce-anxiety-neural-level.

Centers for Disease Control and Prevention. "How Much Physical Activity Do Adults Need?" Accessed April 16, 2015. www.cdc.gov/physicalactivity/everyone/guidelines/adults.html.

Centre for Clinical Interventions. "Assert Yourself! Module 4: How to Behave More Assertively." Updated November 14, 2008. Accessed April 19, 2015. www.cci.health.wa.gov.au/resources/infopax.cfm?Info_ID=51.

Corliss, Julie. "Mindfulness Meditation May Ease Anxiety, Mental Stress." Harvard Health Publications. January 8, 2014. Accessed April 16, 2015. www.health.harvard.edu/blog/mindfulness-meditation-may-ease-anxiety-mental-stress-201401086967.

Cuncic, Arlin. "What is Donny Osmond's Experience with Social Anxiety Disorder?" About Health. Updated February 27, 2015. Accessed April 8, 2015. www.socialanxietydisorder.about.com/od/celebritieswithsad/p/donnyosmond.htm.

Ehrlich, Steven D. "Lemon Balm." University of Maryland Medical Center. Updated March 05, 2011. Accessed April 19, 2015. www.umm.edu/health/medical/altmed/herb/lemon-balm.

Freeman, Daniel, and Jason Freeman. Know Your Mind: The Complete Family Reference Guide to Emotional Health, New York: Sterling Publishing, 2010.

Gilovich, Thomas, Victoria Medvec, and Kenneth Savitsky. "The Spotlight Effect in Social Judgment: An Egocentric Bias in Estimates of the Salience of One's Own Actions and Appearance." Journal of Personality and Social Psychology 78, no. 2 (February 2000): 211–22. doi.org/10.1037/0022-3514.78.2.211.

Gordon, Amie M. "Gratitude is for Lovers." Greater Good Science Center, University of California, Berkeley. February 5, 2013. Accessed May 8, 2015. www.greatergood.berkeley.edu/article/item/gratitude_is_for_lovers.

Goyal M., S. Singh, E.S. Sibinga, et al. "Meditation Programs for Psychological Stress and Well-being: A Systematic Review and Meta-analysis." *JAMA Intern Med.* 2014;174(3): 357–368. doi:10.1001/jamainternmed.2013.13018

Greater Good. "What Is Gratitude?" University of California, Berkeley. Accessed April 19, 2015. www.greatergood.berkeley.edu/topic/gratitude/definition#why_practice.

Greater Good Science Center. "What Is Mindfulness?" University of California, Berkeley. Accessed April 13, 2015. www.greatergood.berkeley.edu/topic/mindfulness/definition.

Harvard Mental Health Letter. "In Praise of Gratitude." Harvard Health Publications. November 1, 2011. Accessed April 18, 2015. www.health.harvard.edu/newsletter_article/in-praise-of-gratitude.

Harvard Women's Health Watch. "Anxiety and Physical Illness." Harvard Health Publications. July 2008. Accessed May 8, 2015. www.health.harvard.edu/staying-healthy/anxiety_and_physical_illness.

Henderson, V.P., A.O. Massion, L. Clemow, T.G. Hurley, S. Druker, J.R. Hebert. "A Randomized Controlled Trial of Mindfulness-Based Stress Reduction For Women With Early-Age Breast Cancer Receiving RadioTherapy." *Integrative Cancer Therapies* 12, no. 5 (September 2013): 404–-13. doi: 10.1177/1534735412473640.

Hopf, Sarah-Mari. "You Are What You Eat: How Food Affects Your Mood." Dartmouth Undergraduate Journal of Science. February 3, 2011. Accessed April 16, 2015. http://dujs.dartmouth.edu/fall-2010/you-are-what-you-eat-how-food-affects-your-mood#.VVeSaGaJXBE.

Jacka, Felice N., Julie Pasco, et al. "Association of Western and Traditional Diets with Depression and Anxiety in Women." *The American Journal of Psychiatry* 167, no. 3 (March 2010): 305–11. doi: 10.1176/appi.ajp.2009.09060881.

Kabat-Zinn, Jon. "What Is Mindfulness?" YouTube video, 2:20. Posted by "Greater Good Science Center," April 14, 2010. https://www.youtube.com/watch?v=xoLQ3qkh0w0.

Kaufman, Gil. "Adele Says Beyonce Helped Her Overcome Anxiety." *MTV News*. April 14, 2011. Accessed April 8, 2015. www.mtv.com/news/1661950/adele-beyonce-rolling-stone/.

Kay, Katty and Claire Shipman. *The Confidence Code*, New York: HarperCollins, 2014.

Lauren, Lynne. *Simply Meditation*, New York: Sterling Publishing, 2010.

Levy, Marc. "Jennifer Lawrence, Hollywood Muse." *Le Figaro Madame*. November 15, 2013. Accessed April 8, 2015. http://madame.lefigaro.fr/celebrites/jennifer-lawrence-muse-de-hollywood-151113-630012.

Marano, Hara Estroff. "Anxiety and Depression Together." *Psychology Today*. October 1, 2003. Accessed May 8, 2015. www.psychologytoday.com/articles/200310/anxiety-and-depression-together.

National Alliance of Mental Illness. "Psychotherapy." Accessed April 9, 2015. www.nami.org/Learn-More/Treatment/Psychotherapy.

Peterson, Dorene. "Anxious or Feeling Down: Can Essential Oils Help?" American College of Healthcare Sciences. September 22, 2014. Accessed April 17, 2015. http://info.achs.edu/blog/depression-and-anxiety-can-essential-oils-help.

Pomfrey, Elaine. "Eat, Meditate, Exercise—Treating Anxiety Naturally." Transcendental Meditation. Accessed April 15, 2015. http://www.tm.org/resource-pages/211-eat-meditate%20exercise.

Rinpoche, Yongey Mingyur. *Joyful Wisdom: Embracing Change and Finding Freedom*, New York: Random House, 2009.

Sederer, Lloyd I. *The Family Guide to Mental Health Care*, New York: W.W. Norton & Company, 2013.

Social Anxiety Institute, "DSM-5 Definition of Social Anxiety Disorder." Accessed May 18, 2015. https://socialanxietyinstitute.org/dsm-definition-social-anxiety-disorder.

Social Anxiety Research Clinic. "What is Social Anxiety Disorder (SAD)?" New State Psychiatric Institute Columbia University Department of Psychiatry. Accessed April 20, 2015. www.columbia-socialanxiety.org/.

Society of Clinical Society: American Psychological Association, Division 12. "Exposure Therapies for Specific Phobias." Accessed April 13, 2015. www.div12.org/PsychologicalTreatments/treatments/specificphobia_exposure.html.

Steimer, Thierry. "The Biology of Fear and Anxiety-Related Behaviors." *Dialogues in Clinical NeuroSciences* 4 no. 3 (September 2002): 231–249. www.ncbi.nlm.nih.gov/pmc/articles/PMC3181681/.

Stone, Dan. "The World's Top Drink." *National Geographic*. April 28, 2014. Accessed April 19, 2015. http://onward.nationalgeographic.com/2014/04/28/the-worlds-top-drink/.

Tucker-Ladd, Clay. "Building Assertiveness in 4 Steps." *PsychCentral*. Updated February 25, 2010. Accessed April 17, 2015. www.psychcentral.com/blog/archives/2010/02/25/building-assertiveness-in-4-steps/.

University of Massachusetts Medical School: Center for Mindfulness. "History of MBSR." Accessed March 8, 2015. www.umassmed.edu/cfm/Stress-Reduction/History-of-MBSR/.

University of Minnesota: Taking Charge of Your Health & Wellbeing. "What Lifestyle Changes are Recommended for Anxiety and Depression?" Accessed April 11, 2015. http://www.takingcharge.csh.umn.edu/manage-health-conditions/anxiety-depression/what-lifestyle-changes-are-recommended-anxiety-and-depre.

Index

thoughts
  automatic, 41, 44
  becoming aware of, 41–42
  breaking into smaller parts, 50–51
  focusing on past or future, 56–57
  internal scripts, 41
  negative, 22
  positive, 57
  psychological reactions connection, 21
  reducing number of negative, 57
  self-defeating, 74
  social anxiety, 22–23
threats, immediate response to, 25
TM. *See* transcendental meditation (TM)
traditional Chinese medicine (TCM), 152
transcendental meditation (TM), 92
tryptophan-rich foods, 170
type-2 diabetes, 166

U
uncomfortable feelings, 74
uncomfortable physical manifestations, 22–23
unexpressed feelings, 22
University of California, Berkeley, 57, 108

University of California, Davis, 108
University of Maryland Medical Center, 152
University of Massachusetts Medical School, 56
University of Pennsylvania Positive Psychology Center, 108
University of South Carolina, 103
US Department of Health and Human Services, 160

V
virtual reality exposure, 69
visualization, 85–86, 88
vitamin C-rich foods, 172

W
walking off anxiety, 165
water, 170
welcoming anxiety, 113
well-balanced meals, 173–174
What is Mindfulness? video, 57
worry interfering with daily life, 18
writing thoughtful letter, 144

Y
yoga, 162

Z
zoning out, 94

Journal Pages

About the Author

HATTIE C. COOPER is the founder of the blog The Anxious Girl's Guide to Dating, which has inspired thousands of readers since its 2013 launch. Cooper's work has appeared in *Calyx* magazine, BuzzFeed, and *The Page Girls*. She is a Northern California native and current Seattle resident. Follow her on Twitter @CooperHattie.

About the Foreword Author

KYLE MACDONALD is a New Zealand–based psychotherapist, blogger, and radio host with 15 years of experience treating social anxiety. He is the creator of a groundbreaking online treatment approach for social anxiety, social phobia, and shyness. To sign up for updates from his award-winning blog, download the ebook, or listen to his podcast "The Confident Mind," visit overcomingsocialanxiety.com.

·

CPSIA information can be obtained
at www.ICGtesting.com
Printed in the USA
LVHW01s0836130717
540829LV00003BA/3/P